Transsolar
Climate Engineering

MW01070943

Birkhäuser Verlag

Transsolar Climate Engineering
Edited by Anja Thierfelder
With contributions by James Carpenter, Helmut Jahn, Matthias Schuler, Werner Sobek, Andreas Theilig and UN studio and an essay by Wilfried Korfmacher

Water

Earth

Air

House and hide are etymologically nearly identical. Both derive from a common Indo-Germanic root. Like an animal's hide, the skin of a house communicates between the inner and outer worlds.

The circular plan of the building minimizes the exterior surfaces and in doing so also cuts heat loss and solar loads. Winding around the outside, thermally separated balconies provide shading as well as the glare protection needed at computer work stations.

From an evolutionary point of view the home is an intrinsic part of being human. Caveman is the word we use to denote our earliest ancestors. Man finds his house, man makes his home – and this makes man human.

The central atrium faces southward, creating an open view of the exterior from within the two-story cafeteria. Air vents on the ground floor and near the ceiling provide good, natural ventilation, which activates the building's thermal mass. To ensure even lighting, the ten-meter-deep offices are lit from two sides since they also receive daylight from the centrally located atrium.

Atrium The Roman house was built around an open, uncovered courtyard, the so-called atrium. Today this term usually refers to a glazed interior court, which doesn't necessarily have to be enclosed by the building on all sides. One extreme form is the integrated atrium, which abuts the main building along only one side.

The most important function of an atrium is to provide the main building with natural lighting and to create a weather-protected area with a more temperate climate. The temperature in an atrium ranges between the indoor and outdoor extremes all year round. This is achieved through activation of the thermal storage mass of the enveloping surfaces and the use of open areas of water and plants for evaporative cooling.

Incorporating supply or exhaust air atria into the ventilation concept can have climatic advantages. Supply air atria – used as fresh air collectors – make it possible to effectively utilize solar gains in the winter or take the edge off high outside temperatures in the summertime. Stack effects enhance natural ventilation, particularly in multistory buildings with an atrium. This makes connecting occupied zones to an atrium good practice because it facilitates nighttime cross-ventilation and overall ventilation. In many cases fire safety issues must be taken into consideration from the start.

Inside the atrium the solar loads absorbed by the interior shading mechanism are vented via a raised glass roof. The canvas shading device is of an extremely light, flexible construction that can be adjusted according to the weather conditions with the help of ropes.

After leaving the trees, primitive man makes the cave his primitive house. As the caveman gradually sheds his fur, he evolves into Homo sapiens. Finding a new coat to clad his natural bareness goes hand in hand with the architectonic civilization of man.

The supply air for the entire building, pre-conditioned by underground ducts, enters the atrium and is blown by small fans into the office spaces via ducts integrated in the ceiling slabs. These ducts also serve as flexible channels for electrical wiring and communication lines. Accessible from the gallery, they can be retrofitted and assigned new functions anytime.

Mechanical Ventilation If fans are used for room ventilation, this is called mechanical ventilation as opposed to natural ventilation. The advantage of this method is a reliable supply of fresh air as well as the ease in operation or regulation using switches, timers, or centralized HVAC controls.

The disadvantage of mechanical ventilation is the technical equipment required: filters, supply and exhaust ducts, blowers, etc. If a ventilation duct has been optimized for cost efficiency, the air conducted in it can reach a speed of 5 m/sec or more.

In order to lower the primary energy input by reducing friction, this speed must be cut by 2–3 times, which means enlarging the duct. Here one must weigh investment against operating costs. Further considerations are space requirements for risers or for installations above suspended ceilings.

The 12-meter-high by 5-meter-wide water wall in the atrium humidifies supply air headed for the office spaces in the winter; in the summer, enhanced evaporation has a slight cooling effect.

Water Wall A water wall, which is generally created by a fixed vertical panel of metal or synthetic material that guides the falling water, provides a large surface area for evaporation. If this water is cooled to 12 – 13 °C in the summertime, the opposite effect can also be achieved: water vapor condenses on the water surface and the surrounding air is dehumidified and cooled at the same time. During the winter, fresh outside air has a low water vapor content. By heating it, the relative humidity indoors sinks drastically. Humidifying incoming air enhances comfort and reduces the risk of respiratory disease.

Water walls do not only influence a room's climate but its atmosphere as well: the soft trickling sound of water can drown out disturbing background sounds, such as traffic noise, or enliven interior spaces.

To create a protective skin between man and the world is the purpose, meaning, and objective of building. The house has become our third skin; we want to feel at home in it.

Air collectors made of perforated corrugated sheet metal are integrated into the façade below waist level. These heat the mechanically supplied air. Venetian blinds offer flexible protection from the sun; light shelves redirect daylight from the skylights toward the room's interior and provide glare-free workstations.

The farther man strays from his place of origin, the more demands a building places on its achievements. Comfort is no longer the sole criterion for a house. Architecture is growing ever more complex and sophisticated.

Solar gains are absorbed by a black wall and are used to drive the ventilation via integrated exhaust air stacks. This also flushes cool night air through the building. A cover of metallic coated glass reduces the radiation of unwanted heat into the office spaces.

Gradually man emancipates his home from its bare natural form. The road from the cave to the house leads us first to the hut. The hut is more of a nest than a house. The hut is fleeting, more akin to the tent, and to the igloo, too.

The north-south orientation of the main façades divides the building into two distinct hemispheres: a fully transparent south façade with solar gains and a semi-obscured north façade. The water basin located on the north side humidifies and cools the fresh air as it enters the building.

Rainwater Utilization Rainwater can be collected from roof drainage systems or other sealed surfaces. After passing through various clarification basins or a filtration plant it is stored in a cistern for future use. The holding capacity of a cistern should correspond to 1 cubic meter per 25 square meters of collection surface. Overall it should be able to provide sufficient water for three weeks. Rainwater can be used for gardens, toilets, and laundry. By utilizing rainwater, drinking water consumption in residential buildings can be reduced by 50%.

Evacuated tube collectors are especially well suited for installation on flat roofs or vertical walls because the tubes themselves can be rotated to ensure the optimal alignment of the absorbing surface to the sun. A collector surface area of 9 square meters can sufficiently heat the building's domestic water.

Solar Collector Dark surfaces absorb the sun's rays and convert them into heat energy. A collector is essentially a specially coated absorber surface that collects solar heat and applies it via closed water or air circuits to a desired use or storage unit. Heat loss from the collector to its surroundings is kept to a minimum by back insulation, selective absorber coatings, special glazings, or even evacuated collectors. Flat plate collectors are most common, also available are the highly efficient evacuated tube collectors.

Germany's climate makes it possible to meet 50–70% of the domestic hot water needs with solar energy, leaving the remaining water heating requirements to be covered by other means, just as auxiliary heating is required in solar facilities.

In the days of the hut, an approach to climate is still lacking. There is only weather – and the elements. The difference between inside and outside is like night and day. Light and air circulate between exterior and interior space. Cold and warm lie worlds apart.

Via an attached single glazing a permanently ventilated double window is created which uses acoustic panels between the panes to dampen the noise level of urban traffic. Despite sound levels of greater than 70 dB it was possible to naturally ventilate the office space by opening the inner glazing of the double window.

The house creates elementary boundaries. The existential requirements of architecture are the same all over the world. It is only the environment that determines the differences in the result. The sophistication of buildings runs parallel with the development of art and culture.

When dealing with historical monuments and landmarks, the new building can only be integrated in a low-key design approach to find acceptance.

Decisive to the emergence of different architectures is not what kind of person one is. Building methods depend on the climate and the materials. The degree of shelter of a people corresponds to its culture.

Made of corrugated metal, the underground duct is 250 meters long and 2 meters in diameter. It cools the building's supply air, especially during evening events in the summertime.

Underground Duct While the ground surface is directly exposed to the elements and seasonal temperature fluctuations, the temperature starting at approximately 10–12 meters below ground remains constant. Undisturbed, it corresponds to the average annual outdoor temperature, which in Germany would be 9.6 °C. It makes sense to take advantage of this natural reservoir for heating and cooling purposes.

An underground duct or underground heat exchanger is a pipe installed below ground through which incoming air is introduced into the building. The greater the temperature difference between the incoming air and the surrounding earth, the greater the change in the temperature of the air as it passes though the ground and into the building. The advantage of an underground duct, therefore, is most noticeable on very hot or very cold days. These extreme temperatures are moderated by the underground duct. The HVAC system connected to it can be sized to accommodate a moderate base load.

Underground ducts generally range between 30 and 200 meters in length and are affordable, maintenance-free, and simple to use.

An approach to differentiating between cultures is to compare and contrast their technologies. Cultural technologies are especially prevalent in architecture. "Show me your house, and I'll tell you the nature of your soul."

The conflicting demands on the building envelope of transparency and solar protection are resolved in a double-skin façade that provides flexible shading and ensures noise protection. Along its entire height the double-skin façade acts as an exhaust air stack, enhancing room ventilation and actively providing for heat removal from the shading devices within the façade cavity.

Even the most magnificent palace or cathedral has its humble beginnings. The humble hut represents human proportions. To build a hut is every man's prerogative.

Large, motorized façade flaps allow night-time ventilation, activating the thermal storage mass with incoming cool night air.

In larger communities division of labor becomes common practice. Building houses is no longer every man's business. The handyman yields to the craftsman. The trade of master builder begins to emerge.

An extensive garden situated on a rooftop provides a buffer for precipitation and minimizes drainage loads.

Rooftop Greening A rooftop garden is a common component of green architecture. Retaining rainwater and reintroducing it into the natural life cycle through evaporation slows the steady trend toward sealing off and paving over our living space. The surface temperature of the green rooftop is very low even in extremely hot periods. This saves cooling energy and raises thermal comfort within the building.

We differentiate between extensive greening with a vegetation layer of 5–12 centimeters and intensive greening with plant growth, including shrubs and bushes, reaching a height of 30–40 centimeters. Through the use of substrate layers with a high water storage capacity it is possible to work with minimal layer thicknesses and weights as low as 20 kg/m^2.

The more a society evolves, the more exacting it becomes with its buildings. New social functions require new architectonic functions.

The supporting grid of the roof rests on four columns. Incoming air flows into the space at the base of these columns, producing a fresh air reservoir up to a certain level. At the top, expended air escapes through outlets in the specially perforated columns. The points at which these columns penetrate the ceiling serve in addition for natural lighting and smoke exhaust.

Stack Ventilation Air that is warmer than the ambient air rises by virtue of its lower density. The buoyant force increases linearly with the temperature difference to the surrounding air and proportionately to the square root of the height of the stack.

This physical process can be used for the ventilation of buildings through the construction of stacks that channel warm, expended air up to the roof. At the same time supply air inlets are necessary in order to let cool outside air enter in its place. The distance between the supply and exhaust air vents should be as large as possible. Oftentimes parts of buildings, e.g. atria or staircases, are employed as stacks.

The stack effect operates well in the winter or on cool summer nights, but fails when the difference in temperature is only minimal or the distance to the end of the stack too short. For the upper level of a building a stack extension or supplementary mechanical ventilation is necessary.

The purpose of the hut is to provide man with a home. As civilization advances, man begins housing other areas of life. Buildings of a higher order arise.

Part of the waste heat generated by the drying machine in this commercial printing house is stored in the ground below the floor and is used in the winter to balance heat losses through the floor. The foundation heat exchanger used here as an active insulation makes standard perimeter insulation unnecessary. In the summertime, the wall surfaces cooled by night air and the floor slab cooled by its direct contact to the ground below serve as thermal storage masses, providing a buffer for the internal and external heat loads that accumulate during the day.

A house rarely stands alone. Building means socialization. Architecture is at the cradle of every society. For protection, communities organize themselves within the walls of fortresses. Cities, too, define themselves at first with walls. Side by side, house upon house.

The completely glazed southwest façade is equipped with fixed horizontal shading louvers that keep the view to the exterior. A distance between the louvers and the glazed façade ensures adequate gap ventilation.

The urban concept, however, is not born merely of walls that protect us against our enemies; every settlement also represents a climate community. The growth of the early city seems chaotic, but if one looks closely, one discovers the order within its labyrinthine building methods.

Along the southwest façade fresh air is sucked in by three chimneys. The chimneys as well as the filter surfaces and the heat exchangers have been sized so generously that no appreciable pressure drops occur. In this way, the stack effect alone is sufficient to provide ventilation during the winter.

The social nature of the urban system reveals itself in the system as a whole, in a creation of the climate collective. A house has four walls. Two houses back to back have seven. Houses grow outward, and they grow upward.

A black wall, a side delimitation of the central atrium, extends above roof level. Integrated in this wall are chimneys that serve as exhaust air stacks for nighttime cross-ventilation at the top and as supply air shafts connected to the underground duct system at the bottom.

A high-rise needs stair space, though it gets by with less roof. In hot regions dense building provides protection from the sun. Narrow streets shed shade. They hold heat during cool phases.

The atrium is the central circulation zone, a space for meeting and communication, but it is also the air distributor. Due to the atrium's raised roof, sufficient solar protection can be achieved by an internal shading device: heat accumulating above the fabric screens is expelled via the black wall without disturbing the occupied spaces.

Like the galleries of an ant colony the convoluted network of the urban community is fueled by economic and environmental motivations. The abundant natural goods in the countryside become rare commodities in the city. People are forced to find other ways of making ends meet.

By virtue of their thermal storage capacity, bare concrete surfaces in the offices and atrium partially clad with wooden lamellas abate increases in temperature caused by internal and external heat loads.

Space becomes scarce, light and air materialize into economic factors. Climate becomes a cost factor. The Industrial Revolution means a quantum leap for the urban conglomeration too. Big modern cities boom, global metropolises mushroom.

Individually adjustable light shelves provide natural background lighting of the interior spaces, even with shading devices in place. Glare-free room lighting provided by daylight not only saves electricity but also reduces heat loads. Given equal amounts of lighting, artificial light generates at least twice the heat input.

The city explodes, giving rise to modernism. In the early phase of the industrial age the environment is not an issue, all that counts is what is humanly possible. With technical materials and mechanical technology man can actually do what architects have only dared dream of until now.

As part of the refurbishing and conversion of the old mill into residential and business spaces, the old turbine facility was restored to be able to produce renewable electricity.

Water Power Water power utilization is a traditional application of renewable energy. With the advent of electrification in the first half of the 20th century many of these industrial plants were converted to electrical operation. Recently a number of these plants in Germany have been restored and with the help of generators they produce renewable electricity that, in 2000, accounted for 4% of the total German energy production and approximately 80% of the renewable energy share. Unlike other renewable energy sources 75% of the hydroelectric potential in Germany is already being utilized today.

Fantastical palaces are built on the solid ground and hard facts of our modern-day world. Sublime skyscrapers pierce the clouds; tenuous towers of steel and glass defy gravity. Ever more buildings are being erected for purposes other than dwelling.

The south façade of the industrial mill is a protected historical monument, therefore the installation of energy-optimized, exterior solar protection glazing was not an option. Instead, an interior, highly reflective louver shading device was installed, which allows the warm room air to exhaust via motorized façade flaps.

Advanced buildings serve as schools and factories, as hospitals and hotels, as capitols and arenas, as theaters and museums, as train stations and airports, exhibition halls, malls, and increasingly, as offices too.

All four façades were conceived as double-wall systems for noise protection reasons. In addition they are also used for natural ventilation: in the summertime, as an exhaust air façade; in the winter, as a supply air façade.

Double-Skin Façade Double-skin façades are typically façade constructions in which an additional glazed skin is situated in front of an inner façade, creating an air corridor that is either continuous or separated between floors. The typical functions of a façade, such as weather protection, thermal envelope, ventilation, protection against sun, glare, and noise, are thus distributed to the different layers. The double-skin façade, if air circulates from or to the adjacent occupied zones, can serve the dual function of delivering supply air and removing exhaust air.

Moreover, interstitial shading devices are protected from the wind. Opaque waist-to-floor areas of the interior façade can be used as acoustic absorption surfaces for noise reduction in the space between the façades.

The issue of energy is currently gaining ground in architecture. He who conserves energy has more of it. He who has energy has comfort too. He who produces energy is self-sufficient.

Thanks to their large cross-sectional area, the exhaust air flaps at the top of the double-skin façade ensure good ventilation in the summertime, thus limiting the temperature rise in the interstitial space above the surrounding temperature to approx. 4 kelvin. In the winter, the awning windows are only opened a crack in order to maintain an interstitial buffer temperature and preheat the required amount of fresh air.

Energy is vital to life, vital to survival. The ecology of energy is vital to the dearest interests of the entire planet. The global community is becoming an energy community, as long as it seeks to remain intact.

Air collectors are used in the winter to heat the supply air entering the north-oriented spaces before it is distributed via the double-skin façade. In order to avoid inadvertent shading of the collector surfaces, the vegetation of the rooftop's extensive garden needs to be trimmed regularly.

Ultraviolet radiation, which is important for a natural living environment, enters virtually uninhibited via a membrane roof. Plants provide shade and act as natural solar protection. Large façade flaps prevent the enclosure from overheating in the summertime.

In point of fact, our consumption of energy has become a critical planetary parameter. In point of fact, we use more energy to drive our buildings than we do to drive our cars. Modern buildings are dependent on the economy of their energy systems.

A three-layer synthetic membrane, which holds its shape with the help of a blower, is used for this extremely light roof construction, providing a high degree of transparency with adequate thermal insulation. In combination with radiators and floor heating, radiant ceiling heating panels arranged below the slender roof trusses produce a subtropical indoor climate for elephants and monkeys, even in the winter.

Though building costs are still the main consideration in investment calculations, operating costs are steadily gaining importance. And usually it is not keeping the building in shape that runs up the bill but keeping the building heated or cooled.

The west elevation shows the building's clear structural arrangement, which is divided into a 14-meter-deep occupied zone with natural lighting from both sides and a glass access zone on the south side.

Use of Daylight Lighting rooms using side windows is geometrically limited. The maximum depth of a room suitable for sufficient daylighting is 1.5 times the window head height. Moreover, on overcast days the luminous intensity is three times greater at the zenith than near the horizon. Buildings with efficient daylighting strategies, therefore, have high windows or skylights and are lit from multiple sides.

Direct sunlight may brighten the spirits, but it often produces glare. This can be remedied by measures such as indirect lighting, floor plan organization, translucent glazing, or adjustable shading mechanisms.

Daylight has a remarkable output, i.e. the luminous flux measured in lumens per watt of solar radiation. Direct sunlight delivers 90 lm/W; indirect diffuse radiation as much as 130 lm/W. That is considerably more than electric lamps, which only give off 10 – 70 lm/W. With natural lighting, moreover, the heat input in a room is notably lower.

The south façade regulates daylight and energy transmittance. The motorized aluminum louvers in the gap between the panes of insulating glass can be rotated and adjusted depending on illuminance and room temperature. The façade, virtually an adaptive envelope, determines the building's outward appearance: depending on the position of the louvers, it gives it either a completely closed or an utterly transparent look.

Advanced and conventional buildings are two different states of matter. The former have matured into technological systems. Modern buildings are responsive entities. Ideally, they adjust to variable outside influences.

The south atrium is circulation area, solar collector, and exhaust air shaft at once.
In the winter, the already warm exhaust air is further heated by solar gains and then passed through a heat recovery system. With a base preconditioned temperature of 15 °C the inside temperature can reach a Mediterranean 25 °C on extremely cold but sunny winter days. In the summer, the atrium is cross-ventilated at night.

Constructive architecture is spawned by technological intelligence. Innovative building materials and technologies allow for building constructions with processual features. Cybernetic concepts adapt the climate engineering of a building to the needs of its user.

For conservation reasons, an energy-efficient refurbishment of the existing exterior façade using insulation was not possible. A strategy of glazed circulation corridors acting as a thermal buffer in combination with a corresponding ventilation concept guaranteed thermal protection according to modern standards.

In an indoor swimming pool thermal comfort is particularly important. A perceived temperature of approximately 27 °C is regarded as pleasant by people dressed in skimpy swim wear. Lower temperatures or drafts have a negative influence on one's sense of comfort. High envelope surface temperatures, achieved through a double-skin system of façade and roof, raise the perceived temperature. Air temperature can be reduced by 2 kelvin, which in turn markedly cuts heating needs.

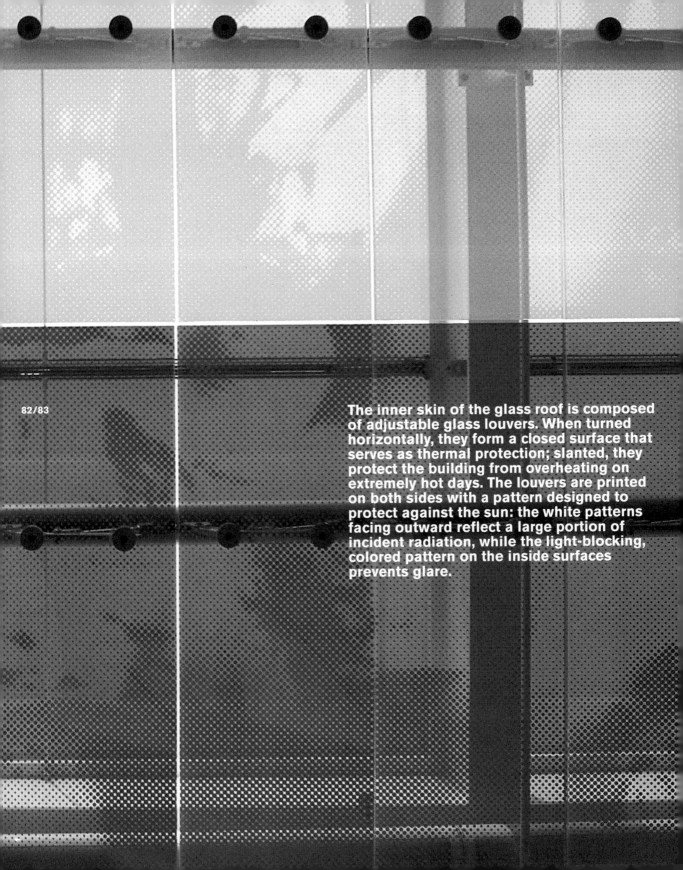

The inner skin of the glass roof is composed of adjustable glass louvers. When turned horizontally, they form a closed surface that serves as thermal protection; slanted, they protect the building from overheating on extremely hot days. The louvers are printed on both sides with a pattern designed to protect against the sun: the white patterns facing outward reflect a large portion of incident radiation, while the light-blocking, colored pattern on the inside surfaces prevents glare.

New thinking creates new architectures – and a new architectonic discipline: climate engineering.

The ventilation of the indoor pool is accomplished using floor vents, the cavities between the façades, and the double-skin roof. Return air is expelled via the north façade. In this way, the interior of the glazed facility gets by with no visible ventilation ductwork whatsoever.

Technologies are subject to innovations. Climate engineering's fundamental tasks are archaic. They are based on the four elements: fire, water, earth, wind.

The ventilation tower ensures exclusively natural ventilation of the auditorium for most of the year. Only in times of maximum capacity use and peak temperatures does supplementary mechanical ventilation become necessary. Incoming air is always preconditioned via an underground crawl basement space.

Natural Ventilation If a building is ventilated exclusively by making use of thermal buoyancy forces or pressure forces caused by wind on the façade, we call this natural ventilation. This method requires façade openings for single-sided window ventilation and uninhibited airflow through adjacent rooms to ensure efficient cross-ventilation.

The fundamental questions posed by climate engineering are of an elemental nature. They are as old as architecture itself. For example:

Cross-ventilation of the classrooms is achieved via a number of motorized windows in both the outer façade and the inner façade facing the atrium. The atrium connects the entire building like a road. Its raised glass ceiling generates an enhanced stack effect. The warm return air from the classrooms provides the atrium with conditioned air in the winter.

What is the building's orientation to the sun?

The sports hall is naturally ventilated via shed roofs, and the supply air is preconditioned in underground ducts. The large glazed areas and both strip skylights ensure good daylighting. Metal grilles serve as glare protection. Venturi wings on the roof aid ventilation in windy conditions and protect the vent openings from the rain.

How does the light change?

A fully glazed building envelope places great demands on the insulation properties and the shading devices of the building. The slope of the roof generates a stack effect for natural cross-ventilation.

How can light be used most efficiently?

To prevent cold draft from the glass roof in winter and to remove solar gains, a transparent foil has been suspended below the glass ceiling. The microperforations in this thin sheet improve room acoustics; the print on the foil or glass enhances shading. The two-layered construction with an additional coating on the interior glass surface performs the multiple functions of heat protection, shading, and thermal comfort.

Thermal Mirror Glass reacts very differently to various kinds of radiation: visible light is, for the most part, allowed to penetrate, while invisible but nevertheless tangible infrared radiation is absorbed almost completely. In a greenhouse, therefore, this heat radiation will remain trapped inside.

In the winter, the floor of a heated atrium radiates heat, which is absorbed by the glass roof. This causes the temperature of the glass layer to rise several degrees; by contrast, there is an appreciable loss of energy in the occupied space. The ideal solution would be a heat-reflecting material: a thermal mirror.

Metals have this property: between 85 and 97% of the heat radiation hitting a metal-coated surface is reflected. Familiar thermal glazing technologies are now also being used to coat synthetic materials. These foils, glass panes, or synthetic sheets remain transparent to visible light, but in respect to the interior they act as thermal mirrors.

How can building materials be utilized for climate purposes?

Roof overhangs consisting of printed glass are used as fixed shading devices. With the exception of the north façade all vertical façades have been equipped with exterior shading. Motorized louvers provide gap ventilation for the double-skin glass roof and regulate the natural ventilation of the interior.

How does one protect a building from heat?

The basic ventilation system relies on the natural stack effect and draws its supply air via underfloor convectors directly from the exterior, whereby the volume flow is controlled via a self-regulating valve. Floor cooling, conducted at night via a small evaporative cooling tower, regenerates the capacity of the thermal mass and removes residual solar gains.

Displacement Ventilation Cool air is blown into the room near floor level at low velocity, thus producing no draft. Heat sources generate buoyancy, causing the fresh air to rise at a speed of approximately 1 mm/sec. The temperature and quality of air in the occupied zones is excellent despite only low supply air flow levels. This is because contaminants in the room are drawn directly to the ceiling and sucked out from there. The advantages of this system are its low investment and operating costs. Displacement ventilation loses effect with strong heat sources because they lead to an increased mixing of the air in the room.

This double-skin system with horizontal baffles between floors creates an open façade corridor that encircles the structure. It ensures proper functioning of the shading blinds, regardless of wind and building height. The main load-bearing structure of the tower is a circular concrete core that simultaneously serves as supply and exhaust air stack. A 250-meter-long underground duct helps to condition incoming air.

How can one control the cold?

The ring-shaped volume of air behind the single-glazed exterior façade eliminates wind-induced pressure using façade flaps to generate a cross-flow. This makes window ventilation possible in any kind of weather.

The external, fixed shading louvers along the southwest façade of the low-rise building create a uniquely characteristic image.

Solar Protection/Shading In the summer, buildings with proportionately large window areas are at special risk of overheating if the openings are exposed to solar radiation without protection.

Fixed shading devices such as cantilevers, awnings, and balconies on south-facing façades block the summer sun, allowing the low-lying winter sun to deliver radiation for heating. The disadvantage of all fixed shading devices is that they are inefficient at harvesting zenithal daylight, which is why adjustable shading elements such as blinds or marquees are frequently preferred.

Externally mounted devices offer the advantage of releasing the heat absorbed by incident radiation into the outside air, thus unlike internally mounted shading devices they do not impose an additional heat load on the building. Another option is the use of solar protection glass, which during the summer as well as the winter reduces the quantity of solar radiation transmitted into the building.

How does one heat a house most efficiently?

Vegetation, water surfaces, and water walls in the inner courtyards of three atria generate pleasant summer temperatures. Large-area glazed surfaces allow a good view of the exterior; expansive louver areas provide natural nighttime ventilation.

Inside the exhaust air stacks, visible signs of a natural ventilation system, there are exhaust air heat exchangers with integrated bypass valves for summer operation. The thermal buoyant force is supplemented by the use of wind caps and – in the glazed areas – by solar heat.

Wind-Enhanced Ventilation If the opening of an air shaft is fitted with the right shaped cap, the wind creates an even greater negative pressure, which generates intensified ventilation. Examples of application can be found in all windy areas of the world, often in the form of so-called wind caps placed at the top of chimneys. Since thermally induced ventilation does not work with balanced temperatures inside and outside the building, wind-enhanced ventilation is an important supplement to natural ventilation systems.

How can one cool a building?

The microclimate directly surrounding buildings can be positively influenced through intensive gardens and water surfaces. Through exposure to these, supply air temperature, moisture content, and dust-contamination levels are improved. Rainwater retention on non-sealed surfaces reduces drainage demands.

A glazed north courtyard provides a means of circulation as well as natural lighting for the adjacent offices. The daylight situation in the corners of the courtyard, however, leaves something to be desired. To brighten these areas the load-bearing structure was clad with sheets of reflective metal. On the north façade, glass panels have been applied whose selective coating reflects part of the visible spectrum: colorful patterns of light are generated, which vary depending on the angle of the sun.

How much heat or cold does use provide?

Double windows were implemented to achieve natural cooling via nighttime ventilation. For security reasons, the windows were not to be left wide open. Here a ventilation strategy of staggering the openings between the interior and exterior planes was chosen.

What comes with daytime?

The relatively small window area of perforated façades limits summer heat gains, which is good for thermal comfort in the summertime. When it comes to taking advantage of solar gains in the winter, the optimal proportion of glass in the façade should be between 1/3 and 2/3 of the entire surface area. The construction of windows as ceiling-to-floor elements provides good natural lighting of the rooms.

Which changes come with night-time?

The return air from the offices raises the temperature of the north courtyard in the winter to a pleasant range. In the summertime, the roof and the façades in the access area are opened extensively, therefore the air temperature at the level of the upper floor only increases to one kelvin above the outside temperature.

How does the influence of the seasons change?

In the summertime, the large air volume can be cooled simply and efficiently via night ventilation. The automated ventilation flaps also serve as outlets for smoke and exhaust heat.

Night Ventilation Given moderate air humidity the ground surface cools down appreciably during the night. The night air thus constitutes a heat sink, which can be employed in naturally conditioned buildings. This principle is widespread, for example, in traditional Arabian architecture.

Safety and security considerations, such as protection against breaking and entering, vandalism, or inclement weather, require that further measures be taken in order to implement night flushing strategies in office buildings. With the help of weather protection barriers, motorized ventilation windows, etc. a building can be cooled by means of cross-ventilation overnight and the thermal mass is allowed regeneration.

Regeneration can only occur if there are sufficient quantities of thermal mass to be activated; overflow openings inside the building and thermal stacks improve results over single-sided window ventilation considerably.

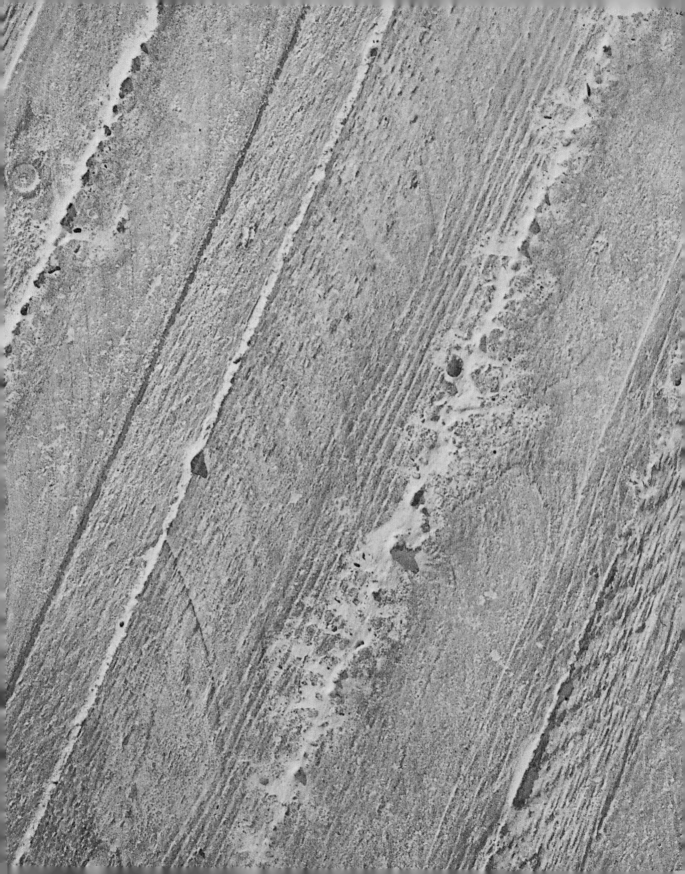

Lightweight construction was used for the roof; the thermal mass necessary to ensure stable room temperature is supplied by ceilings and wall slabs of massive bare concrete in the gallery and cafeteria areas.

Thermal Storage Mass Thermal mass, usually in the form of massive building components, offers a large storage potential for heat and reduces temperature fluctuations in the room. The largest surfaces of a room are the ceiling and floor. These can be exploited as thermal mass, provided suspended ceilings are not used. Moreover, impact sound insulation should be avoided if possible. During hot summer periods even a thermally heavy building heats up, demanding its regular regeneration by means of appropriate measures such as night flushing or building component activation.

How much "climate" is buried in the ground?

Continuous strip skylights redirect daylight into the depths of the room, creating an optimized light situation. Exhaust air outlets for natural ventilation are integrated into the skylights.

How can water be introduced into the system?

Buildings with relatively large glass surface areas tend to overheat in the summertime. Roof overhangs and an operable exterior shading device on the south façade reduce solar heat input.

How can water be removed?

The triangular atrium roof is glazed and divided into rectangular segments. A third of these segments is equipped with rotatable, highly reflective, automated aluminum louvers programmed to track the sun in the winter and deflect diffuse light into the atrium without glare. At the same time the louvers protect against direct solar radiation in the summertime, producing a diffuse daylight situation in the room below.

Light Redirection Conventional side-lighting concepts generate a typical pattern of light distribution in the room: very high values close to the façade, low values deeper in the room. For this reason, even in ancient times buildings made use of light-reflecting surfaces in order to redirect and more evenly distribute daylight. Modern variations are so-called light shelves positioned two thirds of the way up the window. They shade the space close to the façade and redirect light to the room depths by reflecting it against the ceiling.

A number of light-deflecting systems that work by reflecting light off light-colored or reflective metallic surfaces are available. They are usually sold in the form of mirrors, window sills, louvers, or prisms. Technically more sophisticated are optical systems that use curved sections of louvers made of glass or synthetic materials or even holographic layers to deflect light.

Heliostats, double-axis sun-tracking reflectors, make it possible to concentrate direct sunlight, funnel it into the building, and distribute it using systems of mirrors, glass tubes, or glass fibers.

Questions abound and climate engineering rekindles ancient knowledge to answer them. But even more questions arise from the solutions, and these in turn are constantly being used to create new knowledge. For example:

The double-skin façade protects the naturally ventilated offices from noise pollution. Moreover, in the winter, the supply air in the double-skin façade is preheated by solar radiation, while in the summer the ventilation principle of the exhaust-air façade is put to work.

In order to use an atrium to provide window ventilation of office spaces, high air quality and moderate temperatures in the atrium are essential. Both these demands can be met with the help of an adjustable shading device on the roof and summer ventilation via an underground air duct. In addition, the twelve-story atrium acts like a stack whose buoyant forces can be used to cool the building at night.

Why not direct air through an underground duct?

A single-flight staircase cuts though the interstitial space of the double-skin façade, extending from the ground floor to the north-facing rooftop garden. Allocating circulation paths to weather-protected yet unheated areas is an efficient use of the potentials of thermal buffer zones.

A window lets in light, a window lets in air. That's crystal clear. Intelligent systems, however, often produce a more effective air supply and – individually regulated – a more pleasant room climate as well. What's valid for air is also valid for light.

During the day, natural ventilation serves primarily to supply the building with fresh air. The removal of heat loads through night-time cross-ventilation takes place via the ventilation flaps.

Why do we cool and ventilate at the same time?

This single-skin, extremely lightweight membrane roof can be used to span extremely large areas at low construction costs. A special coating on the membrane enables a 70% reflection of incident radiation and an energy transmittance of only 4% – properties that play an important role in preventing overheating in the summertime.

Coupling functions can be synergetic, separating them can make sense. Ventilation and cooling need not be uttered in the same breath – if oxygen comes from the fresh air system and radiant cooling from a separate water circulation loop.

With dimensions of 70 x 180 meters the exterior façade of this hall does not factor significantly into lighting. Instead daylight is provided through the translucent membrane roof. Intense solar radiation can heat the roof to more than 50 °C. Without the membrane's silver-colored interior coating it would radiate down heat like a ceiling radiator. The coating, however, transforms the ceiling into a thermal mirror, reflecting the cool floor.

Why isn't ventilation regulated naturally?

Solar gains in the extremely transparent entry hall could heat the floor significantly. A floor cooling system powered by chilled water maintains a surface temperature of 22 °C – with a maximum specific cooling capacity of more than 100 W/m^2.

We've been blinded by all things mechanically feasible for a long time. It was necessary to rediscover the house as an organic system – and with it the possibilities afforded by natural processes, for example for supply and exhaust air regulation.

Decentralized ventilation boxes along the exterior walls make ventilation ductwork inside the building unnecessary. Based on the principle of mixed-flow ventilation, powerful jets blow fresh air into the room up to a distance of 35 meters.

Mixed-Flow Ventilation With mixed-flow ventilation fresh air is introduced into a room at high velocity and with a high degree of turbulence, causing it to mix very quickly with the air in the room. Since incoming air temperature can differ greatly from ambient room temperature, a high specific heating and cooling output can be achieved. Because fresh outdoor air and stale room air are constantly being mixed, large amounts of fresh air are needed to achieve sufficient indoor air quality.

Why isn't wind used for ventilation?

Only the southwest side of the high-rise was given a double-skin façade with an integrated, motorized shading mechanism. The building's remaining façades are only single-skin constructions with interior shading devices. The high-rise façades are equipped with tilt-and-turn windows operated by a crank mechanism that allows variable adjustment with a lock feature. Windows can thus be left open even in strong winds.

Where wind blows, people seek shelter. But every phenomenon can be both destructive and useful. Positive pressure produces negative pressure. We must not underestimate the power of natural suction for ventilation purposes.

In this low-rise building all exterior façades exposed to heavy noise were given a second skin. The exterior side of the double-skin façades is fixed, but it is equipped with operable glass flaps at floor level and above the attic. In the inner skin, large pivot windows can be opened into the interstitial cavity. In the north the exterior façades do not require shading devices, in the east and west they do, necessitating the installation of louver blinds that can be individually operated by the user.

Why isn't the ground used to harvest energy?

The office spaces in the low-rise building are naturally conditioned by the active cooling of the enveloping building components. Here component cooling is achieved by means of water, which has been cooled to 18 °C, and circulates via a pipe system integrated in the concrete ceilings. The cold water is generated through contact with underground heat exchangers in the foundation piles of the high-rise and beneath the entire underground garage. For structural reasons, a building component cooling system could not be installed in the high-rise itself.

In-depth solutions for modern buildings are not founded on structural considerations alone. Often it makes sense to incorporate the geographical and geological conditions of the site into the climate concept.

The supports of the high-rise extend in part outside the building envelope. Due to the structural demands on the length stability of the supports, they have been equipped with above-average thermal insulation and are even heated in the wintertime – a compromise between the energy engineer and the structural planner.

Why aren't the forces of nature put to use as climate factors?

In the low-rise building the windows of the office façades that face the courtyard consist of two manually operated casement windows positioned one above the other. The upper tilt-and-turn window usually stays closed, while the only 10-centimeter-high tilt window beneath it ensures general ventilation and weather-protected nighttime ventilation in the summer. In addition to the individually operable interior glare protection units, exterior mounted louver blinds also serve as shading devices and at the level of the skylights they redirect daylight into the offices.

The difference between continental and coastal climate depends on the thermal differences of solid and liquid matter. Temperature regulation that makes use of site advantages can save by reducing its fossil fuel consumption.

The cantilevered building components of the high-rise with their good shading capacity are the only source of solar protection for the north-facing glass roofs above the lobby. The entry area receives an optimal supply of daylight.

Why isn't evaporation utilized for cooling purposes?

For structural reasons, the building mass of the new addition was reduced using a hollow core ceiling construction. The duct-shaped hollow cavities running parallel to the façade transport supply and exhaust air. The large duct surface between air and concrete ensure excellent thermal activation of the concrete ceilings, thus offsetting the disadvantage of this relatively lightweight method of construction.

Each of the four elements plays its role in the building's climate. Usually their main impact only comes to the fore through their interaction. Warm meets humid, water turns to vapor. As a result cooling can be achieved.

A wood-chip fired furnace supplies heat to the existing building as well as the new addition. This cost-efficient utilization of biomass reduces CO_2 emissions and is gaining importance in forestry.

Why is building climate controlled centrally?

The access corridors to the conference rooms and overnight accommodations pass behind large glazed surfaces. Acceptance of an intermediate indoor climate in these areas allows for optimal use of the passive solar gains in these buffer zones.

One building, one unit. One building, many units. Two perspectives, which are worlds apart. Contemporary climate concepts do not take a fixed stance. They place the user at the center and adjust technology to fit.

The openings in the ornamental plates supply the cooling tower below them with ambient air. This regenerates the concrete mass of the building at night by means of evaporative cooling. On especially hot days building cooling relies on borehole heat exchangers that penetrate the earth to a depth of 70 meters.

Boreholes/Underground Absorbers The ground under a building has a great heat storage capacity that is independent of weather patterns. Using a heat exchanger system in the form of boreholes or channels integrated into the building components, heat can be stored in or extracted from the earth. This approach is used to diminish peak values for heating and cooling demands and to implement a seasonal strategy of thermal storage.

Why isn't building climate decentralized?

All three buildings are clad in a 4-mm-thick stainless steel skin. A system of perforated sliding shutters in front of the windows is regulated by sensors that react to solar radiation and the outside temperature. Integrated light-deflecting louvers supply the indoor spaces with daylight.

Due to the lightweight roof construction employed, concrete core activation was integrated into the attic wall and gable areas as part of the air-conditioning system. Behind the interior skin, warm inside air cools and sinks to the ground, where it creates a reservoir of cool air.

Building Component Activation A massive, non-suspended concrete ceiling can store great amounts of heat. Building component activation combines this storage capacity with the advantages of a water-cooled chilled ceiling.

The piping in a building component cooling system is similar to that of a floor heating system, except that it is concentrated at the center of the component and is flushed with chilled water. This avoids structural problems since tensile and compressive forces are lowest near the neutral zone. The maximum heat removal rate, however, is approx. 40 W/m², considerably less than a conventional chilled ceiling.

Limiting internal and external heat loads is an important objective of building component cooling systems. Investment capital and operation costs are less than those for conventional HVAC installations.

The pipes installed in the building components can also be used for supplementary heating purposes. The slightly higher surface temperature achieves equal comfort at lower indoor air temperatures, which allows a substantial reduction in air heating.

As flexible as today's architectonic concepts have become is how flexible climate concepts must be too. An adaptive building reacts like a biological organism: its supply systems are centrally planned, its operation adjusted peripherally.

Shafts in the cavity between the metal skin and the glass façade carry fresh air through integrated ventilation equipment, through the space below the raised floor, and into the room via floor outlets. The stale indoor air rises to openings above the windows, where it is exhausted to the outside through the façade cavity.

Why isn't building material also chosen for climate reasons?

The room is lit by diffuse sunlight reflected off the edges of the metal façade perforations. In the conference rooms fabric screens are used to cut glare and provide darkness; fabric-covered frames are employed as mobile glare protection units in the rest of the rooms.

Glare Protection Glare arises through strong contrasts in the luminous intensity within the field of vision of an observer. Effective glare protection is especially vital at computer workstations, where bright surfaces in the room or reflections on the screen contrast sharply with the low luminous intensity emitted by the monitor.

EU-wide regulations relating to computer workstations place strict demands on "visual comfort" and on limiting high luminous density in administration buildings. Workstation guidelines require a view of the exterior from the workplace. Architects want transparent buildings.

Climate concepts must meet all these demands. In other words, they cannot be concerned solely with calculations for adequate shading against overheating, but also have to consider the issue of glare protection: ideally, planning will evaluate both artificial lighting and daylighting situations.

The perforation of the façade shutters allows a view of the exterior even in their closed position. The degree of perforation varies with façade height, thus sufficient daylight is allowed to enter at the level of the skylights.

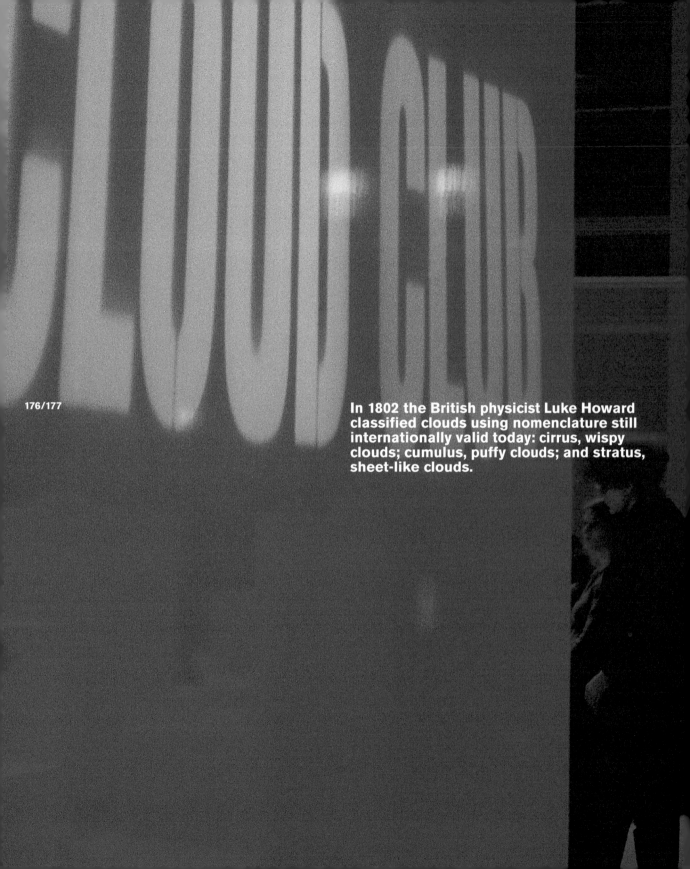

In 1802 the British physicist Luke Howard classified clouds using nomenclature still internationally valid today: cirrus, wispy clouds; cumulus, puffy clouds; and stratus, sheet-like clouds.

Clouds form from water vapor when saturated air condenses on condensation nuclei such as dust, soot particles, or organic compounds.

Modern technologies have made great strides in pushing the envelope of possibility. Now what is humanly possible is being tempered with utility. Innovative building materials can contribute much to an active climate concept.

The transparency of the cloud is controlled by influencing the concentration of the condensation nuclei.

Evaporative Cooling If we leave a liquid in an open vessel for an extended period of time, it will gradually change to its gaseous form: it evaporates. The energy required for evaporation is generally taken from the liquid itself, causing it to cool. If, however, the ambient air is saturated, for instance in moist tropical climates, no evaporation takes place.

Evaporative cooling has been utilized for thousands of years in hot arid climates, mostly with the help of clay vessels or fountains. Today's technical applications usually involve the cooling tower, which uses misting to enhance heat dissipation.

Methods for conditioning indoor air include humidifying warm, dry air, thus provoking adiabatic cooling, humidifying indoor air by means of evaporation, or even dehumidifying room air via cool water surfaces.

Why don't color choices play a role in physically influencing room climate?

The production of artificial clouds requires thermally stable air stratification with a warm, moist layer in the middle. A warm air layer above and a cool air layer below keep the saturated parcel stable.

Cloud On warm, sunny days the air at ground level absorbs heat and humidity. Both of these reduce the density of the air mass until finally it rises. A parcel of air ascends until the buoyant energy has been expended and it comes to rest higher up and in much colder surroundings. Subsequent cooling below the dew point causes water vapor to condense on condensation nuclei, aerosol particles; a typical fair-weather cloud, the cumulus cloud, assumes visible form.

In addition to thermal buoyancy, geographic obstacles or cold fronts can also cause cloud formation.

Color theories are nearly as old as art itself, often they are psychologies. With the help of radiation physics, building materials can be calculated to such an extent that they can provide a pleasantly adjusted environment – in both an aesthetic and an energetic sense.

The outer appearance of the building is dominated by massive solar chimneys with glazing on only one side. They face west and absorb heat in the afternoon. It is not until 2 a.m. that they are opened at the top, thus generating cross-ventilation and cooling the apartments.

Solar Chimney Using thermal chimneys for the natural ventilation of rooms relies on temperature differences. Exhaust air must be warmer than the ambient air in order for it to rise up the chimney. Historical shaft ventilation in Berlin forced the stack effect by firing the ovens at the base of exhaust air chimneys in the summer.

With solar chimneys this heat input comes from the sun. A chimney of this kind is therefore built according to the principle of a collector: glass surfaces are transparent to solar radiation, but at the same time minimize heat loss from the stack to the surroundings. Inside, we find absorbing surfaces that convert the sun's rays into heat.

The solar chimney sucks in indoor air, warms it, and transports it out and over the roof. It generates a thermally powered flow of air masses – without the use of a fan. Equipped with thermal storage mass, the solar chimney can also be used to conduct nighttime ventilation.

Why not apply temperature separation with air?

Solar collectors on the roof heat domestic water and also cover a large part of the hot water demands of the building from a renewable energy source.

From the smallest draft to the most violent storm our elixir is full of unbridled spirit. Air current, when controlled, can act like a wall. In this way it can be used as a building component – invisible, inconspicuous, invincible.

A decentralized ventilation system supplies office space with displacement air. An underfloor device heats or cools the supply air as needed, whereby each user can adjust air amount and room temperature individually.

Decentralized Ventilation In buildings with rooms that have no direct outside link or in the case of especially deep rooms, mechanical ventilation becomes necessary. In high-rises in particular, supply and exhaust air ductworks take up an enormous amount of space. Decentralized ventilation avoids the need for vertical air shafts and allows the regulation of smaller units for individual floors or rooms according to need.

Why isn't natural light deflected into darkness?

Internal and external heat loads have been so efficiently reduced that the groundwater temperature is a sufficient and natural cooling source for building component activation and supply air cooling.

Groundwater Cooling An exemplary form of utilizing local cooling sources for the sustainable heating and ventilation of buildings involves underground resources. Like the ground, groundwater temperatures remain constant, corresponding to an average annual temperature of 8–14 °C. If the capacity of a groundwater well permits, groundwater can be used to cool the building or the supply air via heat exchangers. A recharge well is used to return heated water to the aquifer by surface infiltration.

A cooling machine, by contrast, consumes great amounts of primary energy to achieve the temperatures of 6–8 °C necessary for dehumidifying and cooling supply air. By comparison, the utilization of groundwater, with its higher temperature, constitutes the ideal supplementary method of gently cooling the building via building component activation. Compared to air cooling, the low frictional losses of a water circulation loop also reduce the energy demands on the pumps.

The larger the building, the deeper its rooms. The dark side of the coin is compensated for by new lighting technologies. Recent developments spotlight how elegantly new systems can deflect daylight.

Revolving doors at the entrance serve as temperature buffer between exterior and interior and also help to minimize the pressure differences at the threshold to the forty-story air volume and to prevent drafts.

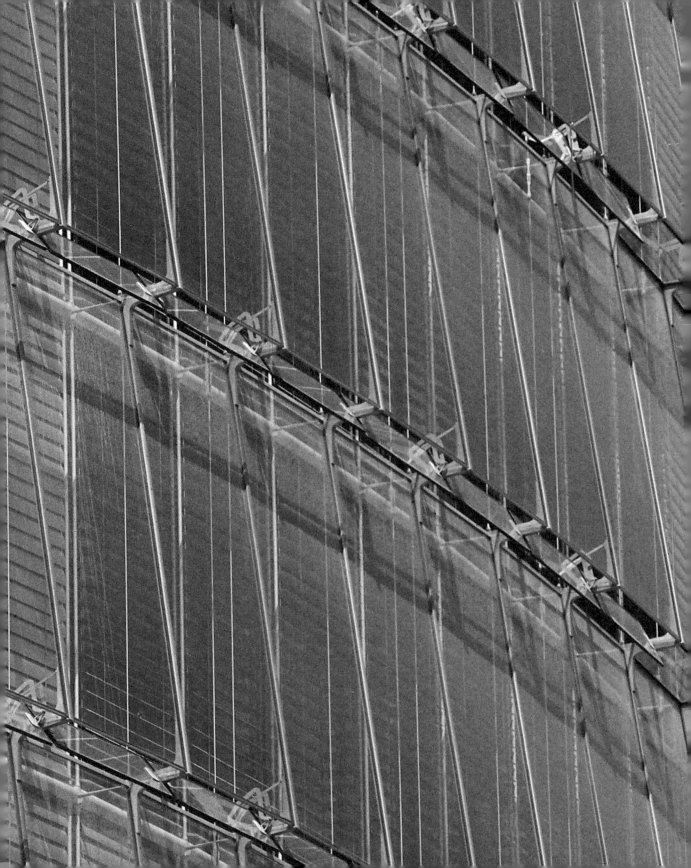

Why isn't glare protection coupled with energy gain?

The external, glazed screen wall enables the implementation of operable windows and provides wind protection for exterior shading devices. The adjustable façade flaps necessary primarily to diminish wind pressure have been sized to keep the temperature level within the double-skin façade from exceeding ambient temperature by more than 6 kelvin.

Solar power has its dark side too. Of course we can combat unwanted light, but it's smarter to convert this energy for thermal application while we're at it.

Nine-story sky gardens sandwiched between the building halves act as unheated buffer zones. They are maintained at a comfortable temperature exclusively via return air from the offices. The interior façades are made of single glazing, the exterior façades of insulated glass, and the raised floor of tempered safety glass, in order to ensure optimal lighting of the inner spaces within the building.

Motorized façade flaps allow optimal heat gain in the summer with the option of shutting the façade cavity during the winter. Depending on wind direction, wind velocity and the pressure distribution on the façade, the position of the vents equalizes areas of negative and positive pressure. Due to higher solar gains, the south façade of the tower was constructed as a shingle-like screen façade that can accommodate larger ventilation openings.

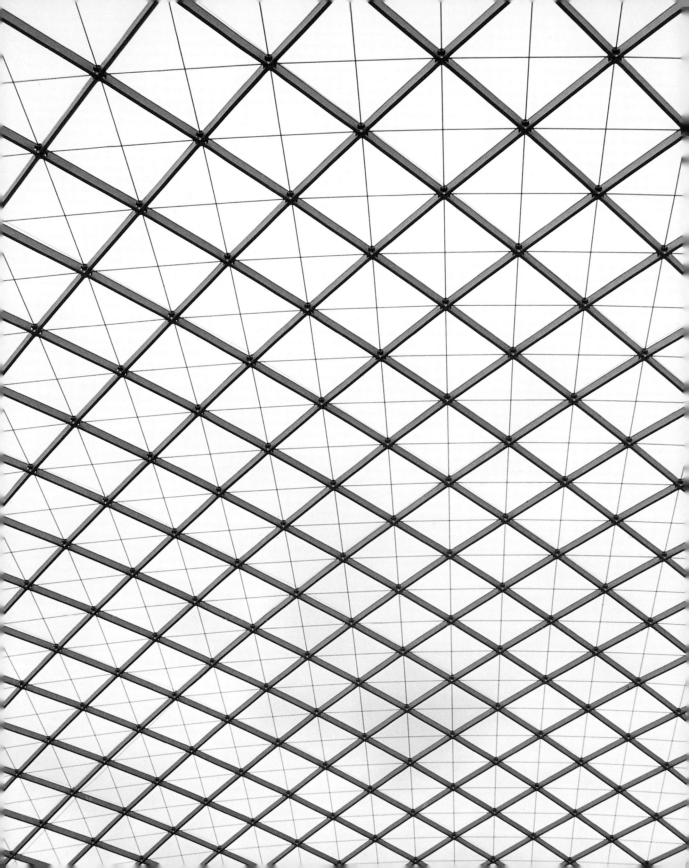

Why isn't climate regarded as an aesthetic category?

The roof of the inner courtyard creates a temperate buffer zone, which supplies the adjacent exhibition spaces with fresh air and daylight. By completely furnishing the vertical roof edge with operable windows, indoor summertime temperatures can be kept to just above outside-temperature levels even without the use of shading devices.

The building climate is an integral part of architecture. It determines to a great extent the quality of the room and influences its appearance. Each room communicates a feeling.

Monument conservation acts preclude options such as suspended ceilings and raised floors, yet museum operation requires full-scale air conditioning. A ventilation system that relies on replacing the existing radiators in the window niches is the only technical option available. Decentralized air conditioning devices installed in each window niche supply the indoor spaces with filtered fresh outdoor air and perform multiple functions, such as air circulation heating and cooling and ventilating and dehumidifying room air.

In the style of the historical façade design of the French Quarter in New Orleans, floor-to-ceiling double wingdoors are planned for the renovation of the façade. Large-surface façade openings increase indoor air movement and this has a pleasant effect when outdoor temperatures peak.

Why aren't problem buildings seen as challenges?

Solar chimneys do not only provide natural ventilation but also expose a building's inner rooms to daylight. Integrated fans churn up the air, allowing occupants to give off more heat: in warm, moist room conditions the thermal comfort of the users is improved markedly.

From a classical point of view climate is a fundamental category of architecture. In the age of high-tech building, climate engineering can help optimize the ecological and atmospheric qualities of a building.

Reducing the proportion of fresh air to meet minimum hygienic requirements cuts the latent heat load, i.e. the energy needed to dehumidify the supply air. Water walls cooled below the dew point of the ambient room air cause moisture in the air to condense and at the same time act as cool reflective surfaces. Moving flaps ensure the necessary mixing and even distribution of room air.

Room Humidity At 20°C one cubic meter of dry air can absorb a quantity of water vapor equal to 17.8 grams. At this point the air is saturated and has a relative humidity of 100%. Warmer air can absorb more water vapor.

Humans do not have a sensory organ for directly perceiving humidity. At a room temperature of 22°C a person generally cannot tell the difference between a relative air humidity of 30% and 70%. These values are perceived by most people as pleasant. In the winter, cold outside air has a very low water content, thus once it has been heated the same air has a comparatively low relative humidity level. This can cause the mucus membranes of the upper respiratory tract and the eyes to dry out. At temperatures above 22°C high humidity is perceived as unpleasant and muggy because these conditions interfere with the body's evaporative cooling mechanism via the skin.

There's no such thing as a problem building, it's just a matter of trouble shooting. Climate engineering is a young discipline in architecture that challenges much of what many take for granted.

Brief rain showers and rapid changes in sunlight and brightness are typical of this location in New Orleans. When it rains, the entire window area is needed for lighting; when the sun shines, shading devices, if possible ones placed outside the building, become necessary. Shutters meet the demands of quick and uncomplicated operation.

The membrane roof of the concourse, composed of PTFE-coated, glass-fiber mesh is dirt-resistant, durable, and minimizes the material demands for the construction of the building skin. In Bangkok's subtropical climate the physical function of the skin automatically implies energy efficiency: the membrane admits approximately one tenth of incident daylight, but reflects more than two thirds of solar radiation energy.

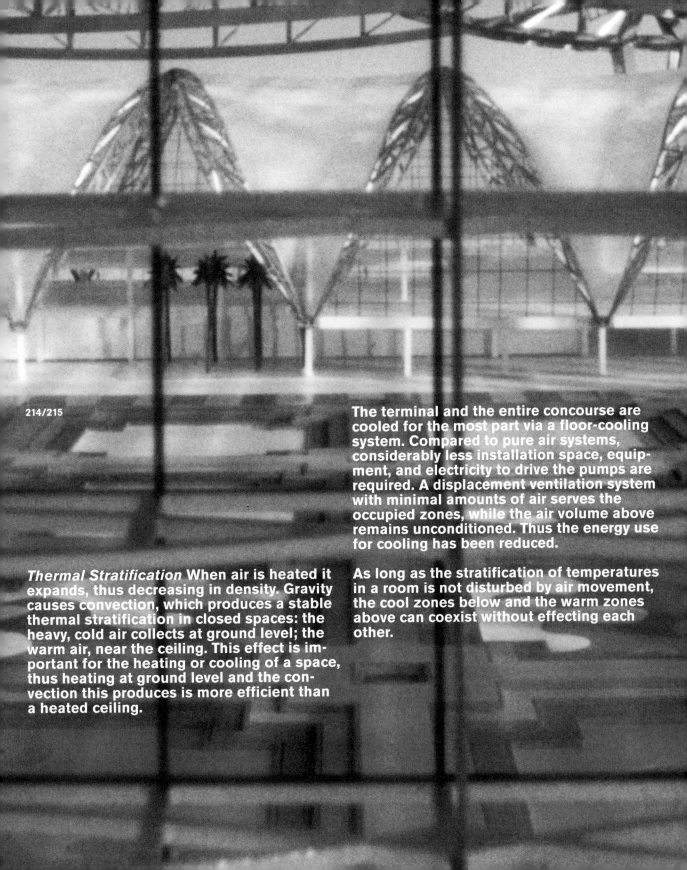

The terminal and the entire concourse are cooled for the most part via a floor-cooling system. Compared to pure air systems, considerably less installation space, equipment, and electricity to drive the pumps are required. A displacement ventilation system with minimal amounts of air serves the occupied zones, while the air volume above remains unconditioned. Thus the energy use for cooling has been reduced.

Thermal Stratification When air is heated it expands, thus decreasing in density. Gravity causes convection, which produces a stable thermal stratification in closed spaces: the heavy, cold air collects at ground level; the warm air, near the ceiling. This effect is important for the heating or cooling of a space, thus heating at ground level and the convection this produces is more efficient than a heated ceiling.

As long as the stratification of temperatures in a room is not disturbed by air movement, the cool zones below and the warm zones above can coexist without effecting each other.

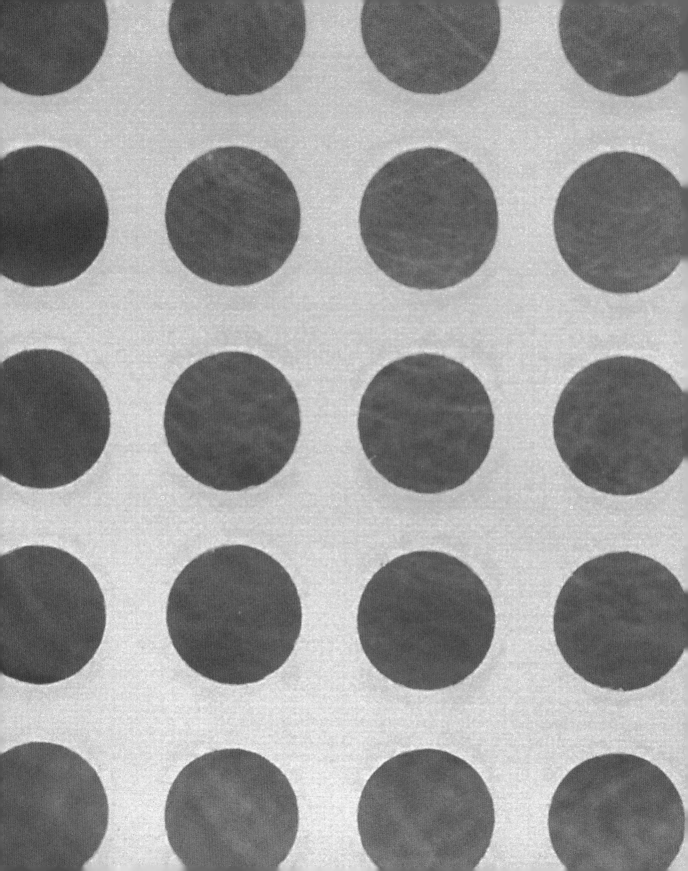

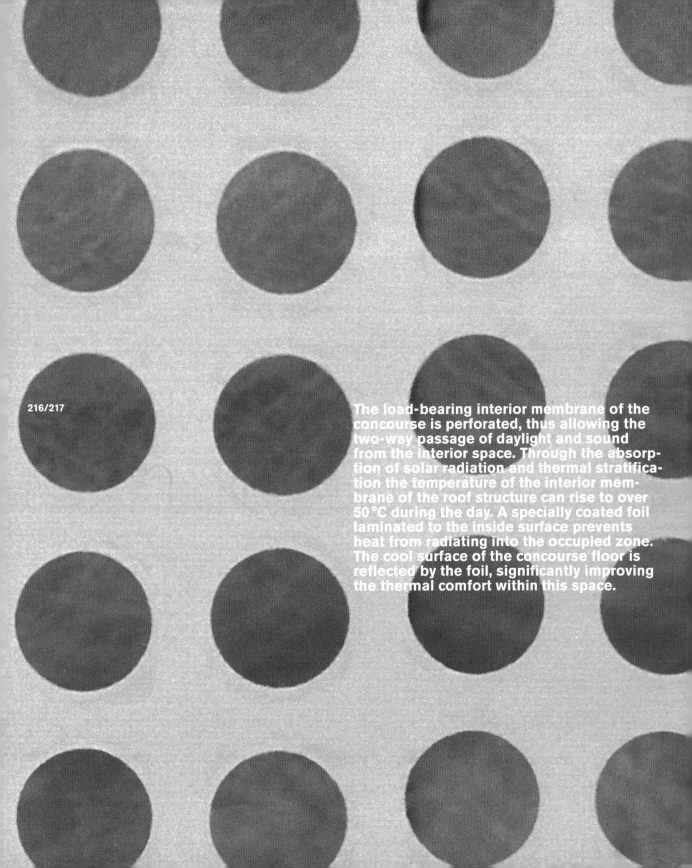

The load-bearing interior membrane of the
concourse is perforated, thus allowing the
two-way passage of daylight and sound
from the interior space. Through the absorption of solar radiation and thermal stratification the temperature of the interior membrane of the roof structure can rise to over
50°C during the day. A specially coated foil
laminated to the inside surface prevents
heat from radiating into the occupied zone.
The cool surface of the concourse floor is
reflected by the foil, significantly improving
the thermal comfort within this space.

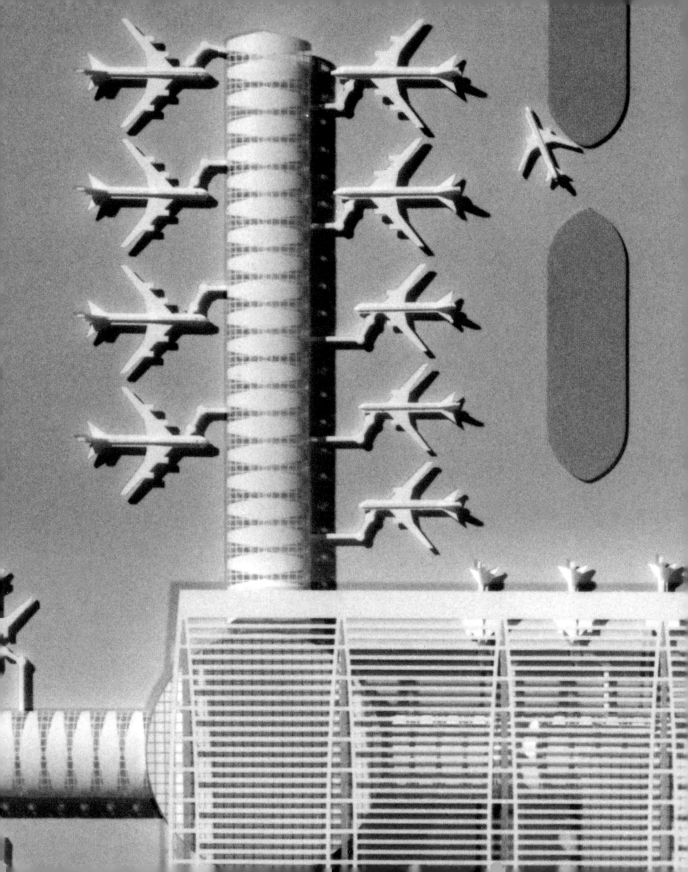

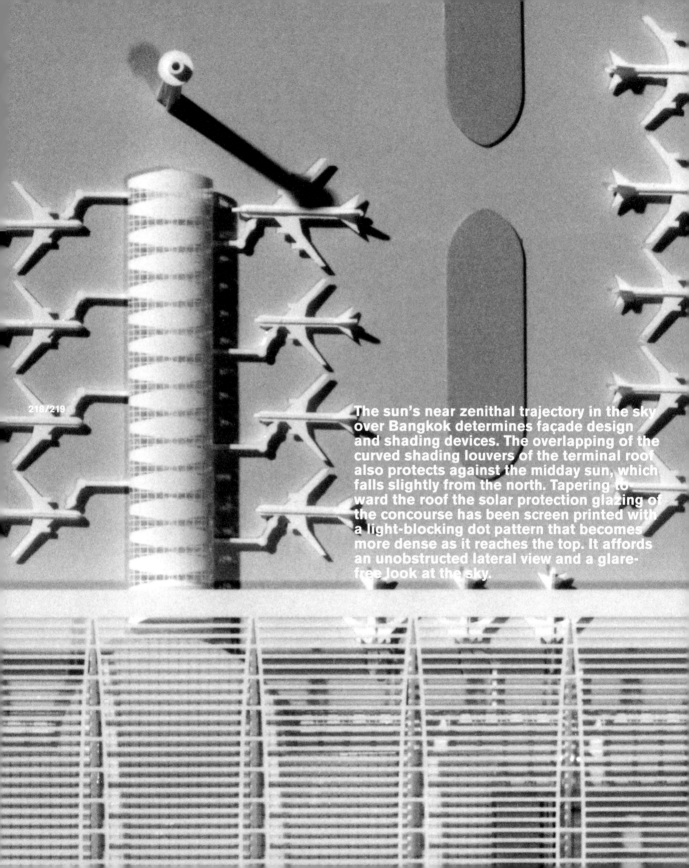

The sun's near zenithal trajectory in the sky over Bangkok determines façade design and shading devices. The overlapping of the curved shading louvers of the terminal roof also protects against the midday sun, which falls slightly from the north. Tapering toward the roof the solar protection glazing of the concourse has been screen printed with a light-blocking dot pattern that becomes more dense as it reaches the top. It affords an unobstructed lateral view and a glare-free look at the sky.

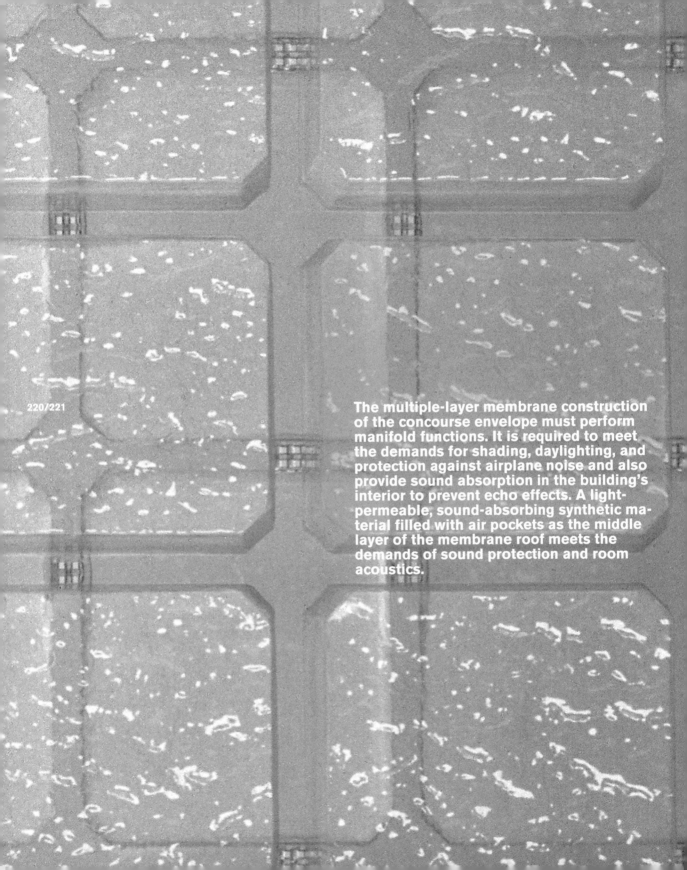

The multiple-layer membrane construction of the concourse envelope must perform manifold functions. It is required to meet the demands for shading, daylighting, and protection against airplane noise and also provide sound absorption in the building's interior to prevent echo effects. A light-permeable, sound-absorbing synthetic material filled with air pockets as the middle layer of the membrane roof meets the demands of sound protection and room acoustics.

In standard building practice simple solutions are far too uncommon. Public awareness of climate issues needs to be fostered. The most important case for encouraging responsible climate engineering is an architectonic, that is, a human one.

The combination of introverted and extroverted spaces is reflected in the façade: closed surfaces alternate with large glazed areas. The outer envelope is like the skin of a car assembled on its frame and propped up against the main levels of the building. Inside, displacement ventilation and building component activation minimize the need for mechanical installations.

The atmosphere of a building is the original goal of architecture. The Earth's atmosphere is the primary objective of the entire planet. The climate of buildings plays a role in the climate of the world.

Carbon fibers embedded in the composite safety glass make it possible to erect extremely high façades without the need for structural support. The fibers also serve as solar protection in addition to the selective coating of the glass, which remains quite transparent to daylight. Its double-skin structure allows this glazing to meet winter comfort demands.

Buildings absorb energy, but they also give off energy. The ecological balance is in order. That's not to say we've merely broken even. Climate engineering respects the environment and conserves our resources. Climate must be regarded as a key architectonic factor.

A spacious atrium creates a light zone between the introverted museum and the open event areas of the conference center and the Grand Hall. The use of selective solar protection glass with 50% screen printing reduces the solar heat load and meets the requirement of a good view of the exterior.

Green is the color of hope, hope in mankind. Let us rely on the four elements. Let us build with fire, water, earth, air. Build a sustainable future. Time to save our hides. Time to save our houses. Let us design climate – by protecting it.

Thermal comfort in the highly glazed atrium is based on an indoor air-conditioning concept that combines displacement ventilation and floor cooling. Ventilation entails a conditioning of the occupied areas only up to a certain height. Beyond that level, higher temperatures are permissible in order to reduce cooling demands.

12–21 DATAPEC office building, Gniebel (D) 1995 client: Grundstücksgesellschaft Gniebel GbR, Pliezhausen

A circular office building with central atrium and exterior façade opening from it like a fan, for 250 computer workstations, employee cafeteria. High demands on glare elimination and removal of internal heat loads. Tight budget.

- Architect: Kauffmann Theilig & Partner, Ostfildern; Project partner: Wolfgang Kergaßner, Stuttgart
- Structural engineer: Pfefferkorn +Partner, Stuttgart
- Building physics: Horstmann und Berger, Altensteig
- HVAC and plumbing: Schreiber Ingenieure, Ulm
- Electrical planning: Heldt &Sohn, Ostfildern

Site factors
- Geographic position: latitude 48.57° north; longitude 9.18° east; elevation above sea level 423 m
- Solar irradiance (on horizontal surface per year) 1074 kWh/m²
- Humidity (1%) > 12.4 g/kg
- Local temperature conditions: minimum temperature -15.4 °C; maximum temperature 33.2 °C; average temperature of hottest month 18.3 °C; mean annual temperature 9.1 °C; temperature difference day/night during hottest month 10.8 K
- Local wind conditions: mean wind velocity (at 10 m) 1.4 m/s; main wind direction 270° (W)
- Local ancillary conditions: rural area; borders on a highway to the south; property slopes downward to the south; detached circular building

Climate concept
- Circular plan to minimize exterior surfaces
- Fixed solar protection in the form of thermally separate balconies
- Atrium with interior, cross-ventilated solar protection
- Natural cooling via night flushing and underground ducts
- Central ventilation with heat recovery
- Supply air to the offices via the atrium and individually through windows
- Bilateral daylighting via façade and atrium

Tools
- Weather data analysis
- TRNSYS for thermal simulations
- RADIANCE for daylight simulation
- 1:1 component testing of the supply air ducts
- Verification of ventilation function through tracer gas measurements

22–29 WAT office building, Karlsruhe (D) 1995 client: WAT Wasser- und Abfalltechnik Ingenieurgesellschaft mbH, Karlsruhe

A four-story, low-energy office building as a compact, east-west oriented structure, designed to be extended to the east. Specific demands included the use of renewable energy and in the building envelope and external facilities open visibility of the client's commitment to environmental issues.

- Architect: Günther Leonhardt, Stuttgart
- Structural engineer: IGP Glasser Hartmann Jung, Karlsruhe
- HVAC, electrical and plumbing: IB Werner Griesinger, Stuttgart
- Daylighting consulting: Hanns Freymuth, Stuttgart

Site factors
- Geographic position: latitude 49.00° north; longitude 8.39° east; elevation above sea level 116 m
- Solar irradiance (on horizontal surface per year) 1045 kWh/m²
- Humidity (1%) > 12.4 g/kg
- Local temperature conditions: minimum temperature -12.1 °C; maximum temperature 34.1 °C; average temperature of hottest month 19.5 °C; mean annual temperature 10.2 °C; temperature difference day/night during hottest month 11.0 K
- Local wind conditions: mean wind velocity (at 10 m) 2.6 m/s; main wind direction 240° (WSW)
- Local ancillary conditions: industrial area; noise from expressway to the east; main façades facing north and south

Climate concept
- Compact building method to reduce heat loss
- Exterior solar protection
- Night flushing via façade openings, exhaust air via solar chimney
- Black wall as solar chimney with integrated central exhaust ducts
- Supply air via façade collectors, ventilation ducts in the concrete ceiling, outlets in inner building spaces
- Fixed exterior light-deflecting elements and adjustable interior light shelves
- Flat-mounted tube collectors for domestic water heating

Tools
- TRNSYS for thermal simulations
- 1:20 scale 3D model for daylight optimization
- ADELINE for daylight simulation
- 1:1 façade collector testing

30–33 Zeppelincarré, Stuttgart (D) 1997 client: DEGI Deutsche Gesellschaft für Immobilienfonds mbH, Frankfurt/Main

Gutting and revitalizing a downtown block of diverse architectural styles and periods to create an administration and service center. Objectives included refurbishing the façade, often under strict monument conservation laws, window ventilation despite noise pollution from the urban environment. The brief also called for decisive improvement of thermal and noise protection and an optimization of systems engineering.

- Architect: Auer + Weber + Partner, Stuttgart; Partner: Götz Guggenberger with Michel + Wolf + Partner, Stuttgart
- Structural engineer: Pfefferkorn +Partner, Stuttgart
- Building physics: Dr. Schäcke + Bayer, Waiblingen-Hegnach
- HVAC and plumbing: Laux, Kaiser &Partner, Stuttgart

Site factors
- Geographic position: latitude 48.76° north; longitude 9.18° east; elevation above sea level 359 m
- Solar irradiance (on horizontal surface per year) 1074 kWh/m²
- Humidity (1%) > 12.4 g/kg
- Local temperature conditions: minimum temperature -15.4 °C; maximum temperature 33.2 °C; average temperature of hottest month 18.3 °C; mean annual temperature 9.1 °C; temperature difference day/night during hottest month 10.8 K
- Local wind conditions: mean wind velocity (at 10 m) 2.5 m/s; main wind direction 250° (WSW)
- Local ancillary conditions: downtown location; noise pollution from Kronenstrasse to the south and Friedrichstrasse to the west; high groundwater level requires constant evacuation of the double-skin foundation; perimeter development

Climate concept
- Winter gardens in the roof area as thermal buffer zones
- Double windows with permanent gap ventilation and optimized shading
- Supplementary cooling energy supplied by use of groundwater
- Glare protection for computer workstations
- Energy harvesting via photovoltaic elements
- Improvement of the microclimate via rooftop greening and ponds

Tools
- Weather data analysis
- TRNSYS for thermal simulations
- Temperature measurements on the built façades

34–41 Mercedes Forum Stuttgart (D) 1997 client: Mercedes-Benz Niederlassung Stuttgart

A transparent sales and event space with a distinctive building form and a 16-meter-high, double-skin façade as a showcase window facing the street. Special attention was placed on sound protection against external noise in combination with natural ventilation and a minimal use of systems engineering.

- Architect: Peter Kopp Architekten, Stuttgart
- Structural engineer: GFI Gesellschaft für Ingenieurplanung im Bauwesen, Stuttgart
- Glazing engineer: Delta X, Stuttgart
- Building physics: Horstmann und Berger, Altensteig
- Building services: Daimler-Benz AG, Sindelfingen
- Acoustics: Bobran Ingenieure, Stuttgart
- Pneumatic wall: IPL Ingenieurplanung Leichtbau GmbH, Radolfzell
- Landscaping: Bernd Krüger und Hubert Möhrle, Stuttgart

Site factors
- Geographic position: latitude 48.76° north; longitude 9.18° east; elevation above sea level 359 m
- Solar irradiance (on horizontal surface per year) 1074 kWh/m²
- Humidity (1%) > 12.4 g/kg
- Local temperature conditions: minimum temperature -15.4°C; maximum temperature 33.2°C; average temperature of hottest month 18.3°C; mean annual temperature 9.1°C; temperature difference day/night during hottest month 10.8 K
- Local wind conditions: mean wind velocity (at 10 m) 2.5 m/s; main wind direction 250° (WSW)
- Local ancillary conditions: mixed area; direct proximity to a four-lane access road; south orientation of main façade

Climate concept
- Night flushing and activation of thermal mass
- Underground duct for conditioning of supply air
- Double-skin façade for removal of exhaust air and simultaneous noise reduction
- Green roof

Tools
- Weather data analysis
- TRNSYS for thermal simulations
- RADIANCE for daylight simulation

42–49 Regionaldruckzentrum PMC, Oetwil am See (CH) 1998 client: PMC Print Media Corporation, Oetwil am See (CH)

A commercial printing house and administration wing housed side by side in two cubes of exposed concrete, steel, and glass. A requirement for the printing house was that future expansion and maximal flexibility for internal arrangement be provided for. High demands on constant humidity levels despite very high internal heat gains caused by printing machines. Natural ventilation instead of the more common fully air-conditioned system.

- Architect: Eberhard Faecke, Leinfelden-Echterdingen
- Site supervision: Gerhard Catrina AG, Oetwil am See (CH)
- Structural engineer: Pfefferkorn + Partner, Stuttgart
- Building physics: Horstmann und Berger, Altensteig
- HVAC and plumbing: Konzmann GmbH & Co, Leinfelden-Echterdingen
- Electrical planning: Th. Meyer AG, Stäfa (CH)

Site factors
- Geographic position: latitude 47.27° north; longitude 8.72° east; elevation above sea level 549 m
- Solar irradiance (on horizontal surface per year) 1104 kWh/m²
- Humidity (1%) > 12.8 g/kg
- Local temperature conditions: minimum temperature -11.5°C; maximum temperature 31.7°C; average temperature of hottest month 19.0°C; mean annual temperature 9.1°C; temperature difference day/night during hottest month 8.9 K
- Local wind conditions: mean wind velocity (at 10 m) 2.1 m/s; main wind direction 256° (WSW)
- Local ancillary conditions: commercial area; high groundwater level; delivery to the east, view from the hall to the west, offices facing south; exposed location on flat terrain

Climate concept
- Cross-ventilation in the summer to activate thermal mass
- In the summer conditioning of supply air via underground heat exchangers
- Displacement ventilation through inlets at column bases
- Upper ends of columns act as exhaust air stacks
- Skylights for natural lighting of the hall
- Waste heat from the drying machine is recovered and stored via foundation heat exchanger

Tools
- Weather data analysis
- TRNSYS for thermal simulations, heat exchanger design
- RADIANCE for daylight simulation
- Smoke test for adjustment of ventilation during operation

50–57 Stadtwerke Metzingen (D) 1998 client: Stadtwerke Metzingen

An almost square, compact office and plant, optical severity was lessened by division and design of the surfaces. Low-energy building that utilizes renewable energy. Renouncement of mechanical ventilation.

- Architect: Planungsgruppe Seidenspinner-Daller, Metzingen-Stuttgart
- Structural engineer: Karl Rumpp, Metzingen
- Building physics: Horstmann und Berger, Altensteig
- HVAC and plumbing: Wallmann und Reiff, Reutlingen
- Façade: Gerhard Weber & Partner, Argenbühl (CH)

Site factors
- Geographic position: latitude 48.53° north; longitude 9.27° east; elevation above sea level 376 m
- Solar irradiance (on horizontal surface per year) 1074 kWh/m²
- Humidity (1%) > 12.4 g/kg
- Local temperature conditions: minimum temperature -15.4°C; maximum temperature 33.2°C; average temperature of hottest month 18.3°C; mean annual temperature 9.1°C; temperature difference day/night during hottest month 10.8 K
- Local wind conditions: mean wind velocity (at 10 m) 1.4 m/s; main wind direction 270° (W)
- Local ancillary conditions: mixed area; moist ground conditions

Climate concept
- Black wall for conducting installation lines (supply and exhaust air, water, electricity)
- Atrium with glass roof and interior, rear-ventilated solar protection
- Activation of thermal mass
- Foundation duct in the form of a corridor between the double-skin walls of the underground garage, for preconditioning supply air
- Black wall as solar chimney
- Light shelves for deflecting daylight and for use as air distributors
- Solar heating of domestic water for the janitor's apartment

Tools
- Weather data analysis
- TRNSYS for thermal simulations
- RADIANCE for daylight simulation

58–61 Ecological Service Center Rommel-mühle, Bietigheim-Bissingen (D) 1998
client: Archi-Nova Planen und Bauen GmbH, Bönnigheim

Conversion of this historical monument, a former industrial mill, into an environmental service center with private living and business spaces. Monument conservation laws forced us to make compromises as to the implementation of the insulation, solar protection, and use of thermal storage capacity we had envisioned in our low-energy building plan.

- Architect: Johannes Keller, Stuttgart with Huppenbauer+Engel, Leinfelden-Echterdingen
- Building services: Konzmann, Stuttgart
- Energy supply concept: IB Schuler, Ludwigsburg

Site factors
- Geographic position: latitude 48.97° north; longitude 9.13° east; elevation above sea level 256 m
- Solar irradiance (on horizontal surface per year) 1074 kWh/m²
- Humidity (1%) > 12.4 g/kg
- Local temperature conditions: minimum temperature -15.4°C; maximum temperature 33.2°C; average temperature of hottest month 18.3°C; mean annual temperature 9.1°C; temperature difference day/night during hottest month 10.8 K
- Local wind conditions: mean wind velocity (at 10 m) 3.0 m/s; main wind direction 270° (W)
- Local ancillary conditions: protected historical monument; detached building; meadows; high-level groundwater; flood zone; south and north orientation of main façades

Climate concept
- Heat recovery (not implemented)
- Rear ventilation and heating of the shading devices, which were placed inside for monument conservation reasons
- Underground duct made of spun concrete pipes for conditioning supply air
- North glazed building as supply air distributor
- Natural ventilation and cooling
- Natural lighting via existing windows with light-deflecting shading devices
- Limiting internal heating loads through guidelines for artificial lighting

Tools
- On-site temperature and moisture measurements
- TRNSYS for thermal simulations, underground duct design and limitation of internal heat loads through artificial lighting
- SUPERLITE for daylight simulation
- 1:1 component testing of the double windows using the collector test facilities at the University of Stuttgart

62–67 Neues Tor am Rathaus, Aalen (D) 1998 client: Wohnungsbau Aalen GmbH, Aalen

A four-story office and commercial building enveloped in a double-skin façade. The brief called for an innovative concept with an outward appearance to match. Offsetting initial investment costs by using natural ventilation in spite of the noise problem. Sponsored by DBU (German Federal Foundation for Environment).

- Architect: Isin Architekten, Aalen
- Structural engineer: Franz Nagel, Aalen
- HVAC and plumbing: Schreiber Ingenieure, Ulm
- Electrical planning: Alfred Stockhammer, Aalen

Site factors
- Geographic position: latitude 48.83° north; longitude 10.10° east; elevation above sea level 451 m
- Solar irradiance (on horizontal surface per year) 1074 kWh/m²
- Humidity (1%) > 12.4 g/kg
- Local temperature conditions: minimum temperature -15.4°C; maximum temperature 33.2°C; average temperature of hottest month 18.3°C; mean annual temperature 9.1°C; temperature difference day/night during hottest month 10.8 K
- Local wind conditions: mean wind velocity (at 10 m) 1.6 m/s; main wind direction 210° (SSW)
- Local ancillary conditions: downtown location; bordered to the south by a four-lane federal highway; south and north orientation of main façades

Climate concept
- Double-skin façade system that is open horizontally and vertically
- Solar preconditioning in the winter via double-skin façade and air collectors
- Waste heat recovery for maintaining comfortable temperatures in the stair wells
- Supply air cooling via underground duct
- Dual-function ventilation system: double-skin façade for transporting supply air in the winter and exhaust air in the summer
- Light deflection via interior light shelves

Tools
- TRNSYS for thermal simulations, design of air collector system and underground duct
- RADIANCE for daylight simulation

68–71 Afrikahaus Dresden Zoo (D) 1999 client: Zoologischer Garten Dresden GmbH

A transparent building for plants and animals at the far end of the new entry building with a zoo school, restaurant, and shop. The daylighting and climate demands are governed by the needs of the plants and animals, construction of the roof skin and building heating were designed to meet these considerations.

- Architect: Mayer+Koelsch, München-Leipzig with Henchion&Reuter, Berlin
- Structural engineer: Wolfgang Feth, Freiburg
- HVAC and plumbing: Eggerichs &Irmscher, Dresden
- Plant planning: Botanischer Garten, Dresden

Site factors
- Geographic position: latitude 51.05° north; longitude 13.75° east; elevation above sea level 111 m
- Solar irradiance (on horizontal surface per year) 999 kWh/m²
- Humidity (1%) > 12.3 g/kg
- Local temperature conditions: minimum temperature -14.6°C; maximum temperature 33.6°C; average temperature of hottest month 17.1°C; mean annual temperature 6.8°C; temperature difference day/night during hottest month 9.8 K
- Local wind conditions: mean wind velocity (at 10 m) 3.8 m/s; main wind direction 200° (SSW)
- Local ancillary conditions: large parking facility on periphery; protected from the wind by existing trees; northeast orientation of main façade

Climate concept
- Tempered floor, radiators, radiant ceiling panels, and mechanical ventilation in the winter
- Plants as solar protection and shade for the elephants
- Generous ventilation flaps to prevent overheating in the summer
- Membrane roof for high UV and light transmission

Tools
- Weather data analysis
- TRNSYS for thermal optimization and calculation of thermal comfort
- CFD simulation for evaluation of local draft incidence and odor distribution

72–77 Innovation Center, Ingolstadt (D) 1999 client: Gesellschaft für Wirtschafts- und Beschäftigungsförderung, Ingolstadt represented by the Hochbauamt Ingolstadt

A four-story innovation center with flexible office spaces designed for temporary use by supplier companies. Objectives included architectural adaptation of Audi's innovative automotive concept, low investment and operating costs, and daylighting to room depths of 14 meters.

- Architect: Fink + Jocher, München
- Structural engineer: Schittig + Schittig, Ingolstadt
- Façade: R+R Fuchs, München
- HVAC and plumbing: Koch-Frey-Donabauer, Ingolstadt
- Electrical planning: Hubert Brauner, München
- Automation, shading, and natural ventilation: Siegfried Baumgartner Solar GmbH, Kippenheim

Site factors
- Geographic position: latitude 48.77° north; longitude 11.43° east; elevation above sea level 368 m
- Solar irradiance (on horizontal surface per year) 1123 kWh/m²
- Humidity (1%) > 12.4 g/kg
- Local temperature conditions: minimum temperature -18.6°C; maximum temperature 32.5°C; average temperature of hottest month 16.7°C; mean annual temperatur 7.5°C; temperature difference day/night during hottest month 11.2 K
- Local wind conditions: mean wind velocity (at 10 m) 2.5 m/s; main wind direction 201° (SSW)
- Local ancillary conditions: industrial area; detached building on level property; exposed to the wind; south and north orientation of main façades

Climate concept
- South atrium as solar collector, utilization of solar gains for heat recovery
- Underground ducts for conditioning mechanically supplied incoming air
- Supply and exhaust air conveyed through ductwork integrated in the ceilings
- Rotatable solar protection devices with light-deflecting functions located in the gap between the panes of glazing of the south façade
- Activation of the concrete ceiling via cross-ventilation, atrium acts as solar chimney
- Robust industrial automation with remote surveillance

Tools
- Weather data analysis
- TRNSYS for thermal simulation, underground duct design, evaluation of different shading designs
- RADIANCE for daylight simulation including visualization
- One-year monitoring of operations to optimize automation and document consumption

78–85 Bad Elster indoor swimming pool (D) 1999 client: Sächsische Staatsbäder GmbH, Bad Elster

Refurbishment of the spa's central building and integration of a new, fully-glazed indoor swimming hall at the core of the historical building ensemble. High demands were placed on thermal comfort.

- Architect: Behnisch & Partner, Stuttgart
- Structural engineer: Fischer & Friedrich, Stuttgart
- Building physics: Langkau Ingenieure, München
- Building services: Michael Huebner Bauprojekt GmbH, Kulmbach
- Electrical planning: Shtop Ingenieure, Helmbrechts
- Façade: Fassadentechnologie Brecht GmbH, Stuttgart
- Landscape planning: Luz und Partner, Stuttgart
- Color design: Erich Wiesner, Berlin
- Project supervision: Harms & Partner, Hannover

Site factors
- Geographic position: latitude 50.28° north; longitude 12.23° east; elevation above sea level 499 m
- Solar irradiance (on horizontal surface per year) 999 kWh/m²
- Humidity (1%) > 12.3 g/kg
- Local temperature conditions: minimum temperature -14.6°C; maximum temperature 33.6°C; average temperature of hottest month 17.1°C; mean annual temperature 6.8°C; temperature difference day/night during hottest month 9.8 K
- Local wind conditions: mean wind velocity (at 10 m) 2.7 m/s; main wind direction 228° (W)
- Local ancillary conditions: expansion of existing buildings; water conservation area with mineral springs

Climate concept
- Curtain walls to create circulation corridors as glazed buffer zones
- Optimization of the thermal comfort in the new building additions via a double-skin envelope
- Printed, operable glass louvers in the roof zone as solar protection
- Night flushing for thermal activation of storage mass

Tools
- Weather data analysis
- TRNSYS for thermal building simulation
- FIDAP for air flow simulation to evaluate room air flow and comfort in the pool facility
- RADIANCE for daylight simulation

86–91 Evangelische Gesamtschule Gelsenkirchen-Bismarck (D) 1999 client: Evangelische Schule in Westfalen e.V.

School as building ensemble with specialized classrooms, auditorium, and chapel along a central atrium, detached classroom buildings and gym. By way of example students should become aware of use of renewable energy. Other aims include good air quality and comfortable temperatures in the classrooms ensured by a simple ventilation concept, getting by without supplementary heating of temporary gathering zones, and as much natural ventilation and daylighting of the gym as possible.

- Architect: plus+ bauplanung GmbH, Neckartenzlingen
- Structural engineer: Weischede Herrmann und Partner, Stuttgart
- Building physics: GN Bauphysik, Stuttgart
- Building services: INCO, Aachen
- Electrical engineering: IGW Ingenieur-gesellschaft für Haustechnik Wetzstein GmbH, Herrenberg

Site factors
- Geographic position: latitude 51.51° north; longitude 7.05° east; elevation above sea level 45 m
- Solar irradiance (on horizontal surface per year) 974 kWh/m²
- Humidity (1%) > 12.5 g/kg
- Local temperature conditions: minimum temperature -10.8°C; maximum temperature 33.4°C; average temperature of hottest month 17.4°C; mean annual temperature 9.6°C; temperature difference day/night during hottest month 9.7 K
- Local wind conditions: mean wind velocity (at 10 m) 3.5 m/s; main wind direction 202° (SSW)
- Local ancillary conditions: residential area; building orientation is indifferent, glass façade of the gym faces south

Climate concept
- Conditioning of air via crawl basement space and underground ducts
- Cross ventilation of the specialized classrooms/labs via façades and atrium
- Use of exhaust air from the gym to ventilate the locker room areas
- Wind-induced ventilation of the gym via venturi wings on the roof skylights
- Light-deflection for optimized day lighting

Tools
- Weather data analysis
- TRNSYS for thermal simulations
- RADIANCE for daylight simulation

92–99 adidas canteen, Herzogenaurach (D) 1999 client: adidas-Salomon AG, Herzogenaurach

A canteen for 1,100 employees, detached, glazed on all sides. A third of the area is to be used initially as a fitness area and added later as a cafeteria extension. In addition to high architectural quality, emphasis was also placed on the optimization of investment costs and an environmentally sound concept for building operation that conserves resources and keeps operating costs down.

- Architect: Kauffmann Theilig & Partner, Ostfildern
- Structural engineer: Pfefferkorn + Partner, Stuttgart
- Building physics: Horstmann und Berger, Altensteig
- Building services: Ebert-Ingenieure, Nürnberg
- Project supervision: Congena, München

Site factors
- Geographic position: latitude 49.55° north; longitude 10.88° east; elevation above sea level 341 m
- Solar irradiance (on horizontal surface per year) 1074 kWh/m²
- Humidity (1%) > 12.6 g/kg
- Local temperature conditions: minimum temperature -12.1°C; maximum temperature 34.1°C; average temperature of hottest month 18.3°C; mean annual temperature 9.1°C; temperature difference day/night during hottest month 11.0 K
- Local wind conditions: mean wind velocity (at 10 m) 2.7 m/s; main wind direction 270° (W)
- Local ancillary conditions: detached, located on land formerly used for military barracks, existing tree population; property slopes slightly downward to a man-made lake in the north; sandy forest soil with a high water table; north orientation of the building to face the lake and administration buildings

Climate concept
- Double-skin glass/membrane roof construction as thermal protection and to improve room acoustics
- Floor heating and cooling
- Fritted membrane as internal shading
- Nighttime cross-ventilation
- Conditioning of fresh air via underground duct labyrinth
- Natural air supply via fresh air elements in the underfloor convector shafts
- Evaporative cooling via the open cooling tower
- Membrane roof as thermal mirror

Tools
- Weather data analysis
- TRNSYS for thermal simulation, design of the underground duct and natural ventilation of the building
- RADIANCE for daylight simulation
- WINDOW 4.1 for evaluation of glazing designs, membranes, and the danger of condensation
- Laboratory measurements of glazing designs and fritting on membranes
- 1:1 component testing of the supply air elements

100–105 Trendpark service center Neckarsulm (D) 1999 client: ROSEA Grundstücksvermietungsgesellschaft mbH & Co. Objekt Neckarsulm KG

A four-part building complex consisting of a 186-meter-long, four-story, crescent-shaped low-rise building with three tangential office beams arranged vertically and an 80-meter-high, eighteen-story office tower. The brief called for keeping technical equipment as simple as possible, including doing without mechanical cooling and window ventilation even on the upper floors of the office tower.

- Architect: Ziltz + Partner, Esslingen
- Structural engineer: Lichti & Laig, Moosbach
- Building physics: GN Bauphysik, Stuttgart
- HVAC, electrical and plumbing: Schreiber Ingenieure, Ulm

Site factors
- Geographic position: latitude 49.19° north; longitude 9.23° east; elevation above sea level 180 m
- Solar irradiance (on horizontal surface per year) 1074 kWh/m²
- Humidity (1%) > 12.4 g/kg
- Local temperature conditions: minimum temperature -15.4°C; maximum temperature 33.2°C; average temperature of hottest month 18.3°C; mean annual temperature 9.1°C; temperature difference day/night during hottest month 10.8 K
- Local wind conditions: mean wind velocity (at 10 m) 2.0 m/s; main wind direction 240° (WSW)
- Local ancillary conditions: industrial area; noise from the southeast and southwest due to motorway interchange; height difference of 2 meters had to be overcome to level the site; circular office tower, low-rise building with crescent looking north, office beams with east and west façades

Climate concept
- Office tower with double-skin façade separated by floor, but open around the circumference to eliminate wind pressure
- Motorized solar protection devices in the double-skin façade
- Low-rise with fixed, exterior shading
- Concrete ceilings as thermal storage
- Underground ducts made of spun concrete
- Central concrete shaft as main load-bearing element transports supply and exhaust air
- Supply air distribution in raised floor, hall accumulation of exhaust air
- Aerodynamic design of stack extension for wind-enhanced exhaust of air
- Daylighting provided by light shelves and motorized skylight

Tools
- TRNSYS for thermal simulation and design of underground ducts
- FIDAP for simulation of room air flow and detailing of the double-skin façade
- RADIANCE for daylight simulation and evaluation of potential glare risk to drivers

106–111 Weleda new administration building, Schwäbisch Gmünd (D) 2000 client: Weleda AG, Schwäbisch Gmünd

A four-story twin structure consisting of the new administration building and a multipurpose hall strongly reflecting anthroposophical formal language and color choice. Largely closed to the federal highway to the northwest, oriented towards the company garden to the southeast. High demands in respect to natural lighting and ventilation.

- Architect: bpr architektur und design, Stuttgart
- Structural engineer: Wickbold und Schmidt, Stuttgart
- Building physics: Bayer Ingenieure, Fellbach
- HVAC, electrical and plumbing: RCI, München

Site factors
- Geographic position: latitude 48.80° north; longitude 9.78° east; elevation above sea level 327 m
- Solar irradiance (on horizontal surface per year) 1074 kWh/m²
- Humidity (1%) > 12.4 g/kg
- Local temperature conditions: minimum temperature -15.4°C; maximum temperature 33.2°C; average temperature of hottest month 18.3°C; mean annual temperature 9.1°C; temperature difference day/night during hottest month 10.8 K
- Local wind conditions: mean wind velocity (at 10 m) 1.1 m/s; main wind direction 240° (WSW)
- Local ancillary conditions: mixed area; noise and air pollution from federal highway to the northwest; company garden to the southwest; groundwater well; southeast and northwest oriented main façades

Climate concept
- Glass roofs with light grilles as solar protection
- Underground ducts for conditioning supply air
- Activation of the ceilings via cross-ventilation
- Supply air courtyards with water walls fed from groundwater well
- Supply air circulation via halls, ventilation flaps integrated into door frames
- Stale air expelled through exhaust air ducts integrated in the ceilings
- Exhaust air collectors lead to exhaust air stacks with chimney caps, expelling air with the help of solar gains
- Heat recovery via a distributed system

Tools
- On-site air quality and noise level monitoring
- TRNSYS for thermal simulation, design of underground duct, shading, and water wall
- EES model for designing hydraulics
- SUPERLITE for daylight simulation
- 1:1 component testing of the fan
- 1:3 component testing of the wind cap
- 1:1 component testing of the heat exchangers

112–119 Extension of the Ministry of Foreign Affairs, Berlin (D) 2000 client: Bundesamt für Bauwesen und Raumordnung

Extension of the German Foreign Ministry for 770 employees. Massive monolith with an envelope made of light-colored travertine, conventional façade fenestration, strip windows, and three large reentrant courtyards. In Germany public buildings are not supposed to be air conditioned. The brief, therefore, called for the use of natural alternatives for optimizing thermal comfort. Natural lighting of the office spaces was also an objective as were provisions for increased security.

- Architect: Müller Reimann Architekten, Berlin
- Structural engineer: GSE Ingenieurgesellschaft, Berlin
- Special construction North Hall: Schlaich Bergermann und Partner, Stuttgart
- Building physics: Axel C. Rahn, Berlin
- Building services: Alhäuser +König, Hachenburg
- Glass art: James Carpenter Design Associates, New York (USA)

Site factors
- Geographic position: latitude 52.52° north; longitude 13.40° east; elevation above sea level 34 m
- Solar irradiance (on horizontal surface per year) 996 kWh/m²
- Humidity (1%) > 12.1 g/kg
- Local temperature conditions: minimum temperature -12.2°C; maximum temperature 33.8°C; average temperature of hottest month 17.9°C; mean annual temperature 8.7°C; temperature difference day/night during hottest month 9.3 K
- Local wind conditions: mean wind velocity (at 10 m) 4.1 m/s; main wind direction 202° (SSW)
- Local ancillary conditions: downtown location on the banks of the Spree, large open areas; close to the abandoned, existing spaces of the former Reichsbank; main entry faces north

Climate concept
- North oriented, six-story patio as buffer zone
- Permanent rear-ventilated double window that allows window ventilation with heightened security
- Night flushing

Tools
- Weather data analysis
- TRNSYS for thermal simulation

120–127 Rotebühl canteen, Stuttgart (D) 2001 client: Land Baden-Württemberg, represented by Staatliche Vermögens- und Hochbauamt Stuttgart

A transparent cafeteria building in the shape of a butterfly with a full kitchen and a dining room large enough for 250 people. Objectives were to make use of the waste heat from a neighboring computer center, rely as little as possible on fossil fuels, and operate the building without the need for mechanical cooling.

- Architect: Hochbauamt Stuttgart
- Structural engineer: IB Schreiber, Stuttgart
- Building services MEP: Klett-Ingenieure, Fellbach

Site factors
- Geographic position: latitude 48.76° north; longitude 9.18° east; elevation above sea level 359 m
- Solar irradiance (on horizontal surface per year) 1074 kWh/m²
- Humidity (1%) > 12.4 g/kg
- Local temperature conditions: minimum temperature -15.4°C; maximum temperature 33.2°C; average temperature of hottest month 18.3°C; mean annual temperature 9.1°C; temperature difference day/night during hottest month 10.8 K
- Local wind conditions: mean wind velocity (at 10 m) 2.5 m/s; main wind direction 250° (WSW)
- Local ancillary conditions: downtown location; south-southeast orientation of main façade

Climate concept
- Supply air preconditioning via underground duct
- Activation of thermal mass
- Exterior shading devices and roof overhangs
- Natural cooling via night flushing and underground duct
- Utilization of waste heat from the computer center for heating

Tools
- Weather data analysis
- TRNSYS for thermal simulations
- RADIANCE for daylight simulation

128–137 Prisma administration center, Frankfurt/Main (D) 2001 client: HochTief Projektentwicklung GmbH, Frankfurt/Main

A representative, eleven-story administration building as a compact block construction situated on a triangular plot: two massive beams and one double-skin glazed office beam surround a central atrium. The brief called for an energy-optimized, naturally ventilated building.

- Architect: Auer + Weber + Partner, Stuttgart, Partner: Götz Guggenberger
- Structural engineer, design phases 1-3: Mayr + Ludescher, Stuttgart
- Structural engineer, design phases 4-9: HochTief, Frankfurt/Main
- Building physics: Bobran Ingenieure, Stuttgart
- HVAC and plumbing, design phases 1-3: Rentschler & Riedesser, Filderstadt
- HVAC and plumbing, design phases 4-9: HL-Technik, Frankfurt/Main
- Electrical planning, design phases 1-3: Gackstatter und Partner, Stuttgart
- Electrical planning, design phases 4-9: K. Dörflinger GmbH, Auendorf
- Artificial sky: Andres Ingenieure, Hamburg
- Project supervision: HochTief Projektentwicklung GmbH, Frankfurt/Main

Site factors
- Geographic position: latitude 50.2° north; longitude 8.68° east; elevation above sea level 113 m
- Solar irradiance (on horizontal surface per year) 1027 kWh/m²
- Humidity (1%) > 12.6 g/kg
- Local temperature conditions: minimum temperature -12.1°C; maximum temperature 34.1°C; average temperature of hottest month 18.6°C; mean annual temperature 9.9°C; temperature difference day/night during hottest month 11.0 K
- Local wind conditions: mean wind velocity (at 10 m) 3.3 m/s; main wind direction 227° (SW)
- Local ancillary conditions: office suburb of Frankfurt-Niederrad; traffic noise

Climate concept
- Underground duct as foundation duct
- Underground heat exchanger
- Use of concrete core to maintain comfortable temperatures in the building tips
- Natural ventilation and nighttime ventilation
- Atrium and double-skin façade with a dual-function ventilation system for summer and winter operation
- Combined shading and light-deflecting louvers on the glass roof

Tools
- Weather data analysis
- TRNSYS for thermal simulation
- COMIS for hydraulic simulation
- 1:1 mock-up of a triaxial office with a double-skin façade
- FIDAP for air flow simulation for atrium and offices
- RADIANCE for daylight simulation
- 1:100 scale model for measuring the light distribution in the atrium in the artificial sky

138–145 Shanghai International Expo Center (CN) 2001 client: Joint Venture SNIEC, Shanghai New International Expo Center, Shanghai Pudong Development Company, Messe München, Messe Düsseldorf, Messe Hannover

A transparent entry hall, which is glazed on all sides, and four exhibition halls with clear span membrane roofs as the first building phase of a new fairgrounds which will have a total of 17 exhibition halls and an exhibition area of nearly 200,000 m². Very tight budget and time schedule. Objectives include a natural overall lighting situation during installation and dismantling phases and a ventilation system without visible ductwork inside the halls.

- Architect: Murphy/Jahn, Chicago (USA)
- Structural engineer: Werner Sobek Ingenieure, Stuttgart
- HVAC and plumbing: Schreiber Ingenieure, Ulm
- Electrical planning: Werner Schwarz Ingenieure, Stuttgart
- Building physics: Horstmann und Berger, Altensteig

Site factors
- Geographic position: latitude 31.15° north; longitude 121.40° east; elevation above sea level 6 m
- Solar irradiance (on horizontal surface per year) 1241 kWh/m²
- Humidity (1%) > 22.4 g/kg
- Local temperature conditions: minimum temperature -6.0°C; maximum temperature 36.6°C; average temperature of hottest month 28.5°C; mean annual temperature 16.6°C; temperature difference day/night during hottest month 6.4 K
- Local wind conditions: mean wind velocity (at 10 m) 3.0 m/s; main wind direction 98° (E)
- Local ancillary conditions: reclaimed meadow, very high water table; south and north orientation of the main façades of the exhibition halls

Climate concept
- Entry halls with floor cooling and cross-ventilation
- Single-skin membrane roof with a low-e coating on the inside and an extremely reduced degree of transmission as thermal protection in the summer
- Natural ventilation of the administration and sales spaces on the façade side
- Decentralized mechanical ventilation boxes with powerful long-distance jets along the exterior walls

Tools
- Weather data analysis
- TRNSYS for thermal simulations and cooling load calculations
- RADIANCE for daylight simulation
- Membrane measurements in respect to transmission and low-e effect
- Physical daylighting model
- 1:1 component testing of the ventilation equipment
- FIDAP for air flow simulation of the long-distance jets

146–157 Nord/LB Administration center, Hannover (D) 2002 client: Norddeutsche Landesbank Girozentrale, Hannover

A transparent office complex with a dazzling seventeen-story high-rise and a compact block construction not exceeding seven stories that wraps around a generous inner courtyard. Environmentally sound measures were to be implemented while keeping within financially justifiable bounds. The objective was to comply with the thermal protection regulations in place at the time. One specific aim was to do without room air conditioning whenever possible.

- Architect: Behnisch, Behnisch & Partner, Stuttgart
- Structural engineer: Arge Wetzel + von Seht, Hamburg; Pfefferkorn + Partner, Stuttgart
- Façade: Erich Mosbacher, Friedrichshafen
- Building physics: Horstmann und Berger, Altensteig
- Building services MEP: ArgeTGA, Becker & Becker, Braunschweig; Lindhorst, Braunschweig; Grabe, Hannover; Taube-Göerz-Liegat, Hannover; coordinator: Gierke, Braunschweig
- Lighting engineering: Bartenbach Lichtlabor, Aldrans/Innsbruck (A)
- Project supervision: NILEG, Hannover

Site factors
- Geographic position: latitude 52.37° north; longitude 9.72° east; elevation above sea level 63 m
- Solar irradiance (on horizontal surface per year) 934 kWh/m²
- Humidity (1%) > 12.4 g/kg
- Local temperature conditions: minimum temperature -13.1°C; maximum temperature 32.5°C; average temperature of hottest month 16.8°C; mean annual temperature 8.7°C; temperature difference day/night during hottest month 10.4 K
- Local wind conditions: mean wind velocity (at 10 m) 4.0 m/s; main wind direction 260° (WSW)
- Local ancillary conditions: downtown location beside a 6-lane street

Climate concept
- Underground heat exchangers for seasonal hot and cold thermal storage
- Exterior solar protection with optimized daylight redirection
- Building component cooling
- Window ventilation for overall ventilation as well as night flushing, partially in combination with double-skin façades
- Vacuum tube collectors for hot water
- Absorption cooling machine

Tools
- Weather data analysis
- TRNSYS for thermal simulations
- TRNSPILE for the sizing of the underground heat exchanger/building component activation systems
- FIDAP for air flow simulations of the double-skin façades and halls
- RADIANCE for shading projections
- 1:20 sectional model for visualizing air flow

158–163 Center for Family, Environment, and Culture, Kloster Roggenburg (D) 2002 client: Kloster Roggenburg

A two-story vocational training center with lodging for 120 visitors, convent restaurant, lecture halls and labs, arranged around the inner courtyard of this historical convent. This training center for environmental issues wanted to have an environmentally sound building as a way of practicing what it preaches. Further objectives were a high degree of thermal comfort, daylight and air quality. Construction was sponsored by the German Federal Foundation for the Environment.

- Architect: Prof. Dr. Schwarz Grözinger Wagner, Memmingen
- Structural engineer: Demuth + Müller, Neusäß-Hammel
- HVAC and plumbing, design phases 1-3: Silberhorn Ingenieure, Augsburg
- HVAC and plumbing, design phases 4-9: Josef & Thomas Bauer, Unterschleißheim
- Project supervision: Max Meixner, Augsburg

Site factors
- Geographic position: latitude 48.28° north; longitude 10.23° east; elevation above sea level 538 m
- Solar irradiance (on horizontal surface per year) 1123 kWh/m²
- Humidity (1%) > 12.4 g/kg
- Local temperature conditions: minimum temperature -18.6°C; maximum temperature 32.5°C; average temperature of hottest month 16.7°C; mean annual temperature 7.5°C; temperature difference day/night during hottest month 11.2 K
- Local wind conditions: mean wind velocity (at 10 m) 3.0 m/s; main wind direction 225° (SW)
- Local ancillary conditions: periphery location; detached building; site with gentle slope

Climate concept
- Hollow core ceiling construction for horizontal air distribution and activation of thermal mass
- Displacement ventilation system with a controlled air supply and heat recovery
- Cooling with well water
- Wood-chip fired furnace

Tools
- Weather data analysis
- TRNSYS for thermal simulation
- RADIANCE for daylight simulation

164–175 Südwestmetall new administration building, Reutlingen (D) 2002 client: Südwestmetall Verband der Metall- und Elektroindustrie e.V., Freiburg im Breisgau

A three-part building ensemble with representative office, conference, and training classrooms formally integrated in the existing environment of the building structure. The open exhibition of the qualities of the metal construction trade and the creation of an extraordinary building were just as much a part of the brief as the functional optimization of the rooms to correspond with the expected purposes, placing special emphasis on an integrated, environmental building concept, and a complete renunciation of the use of mechanical cooling.

- Architect: Allmann Sattler Wappner, München
- Structural engineer: Werner Sobek Ingenieure, Stuttgart
- Building physics: Horstmann und Berger, Altensteig
- HVAC, plumbing and refrigeration: Schreiber Ingenieure, Ulm
- Electrical planning: Werner Schwarz Ingenieure, Stuttgart
- Façade: R+R Fuchs, München
- Landscape planning: Realgrün, München

Site factors
- Geographic position: latitude 48.48° north; longitude 9.22° east; elevation above sea level 408 m
- Solar irradiance (on horizontal surface per year) 1074 kWh/m²
- Humidity (1%) > 12.4 g/kg
- Local temperature conditions: minimum temperature -15.4°C; maximum temperature 33.2°C; average temperature of hottest month 18.3°C; mean annual temperature 9.1°C; temperature difference day/night during hottest month 10.8 K
- Local wind conditions: mean wind velocity (at 10 m) 1.4 m/s; main wind direction 270° (W)
- Local ancillary conditions: downtown residential area; claystone with the saturated zone starting at 4 m below ground surface

Climate concept
- Building component activation of the ceilings on each floor
- Exterior solar protection via perforated stainless steel sliding shutters
- Wall component cooling in the training and conference areas
- Concrete core activation via cooling tower and boreholes
- Displacement ventilation system with decentralized supply air units
- Exhaust ductwork in the double-skin metal façade

Tools
- Weather data analysis
- TRNSYS for thermal simulations
- System simulation of ventilation system, concrete core activation, cooling tower, and boreholes
- RADIANCE for daylight simulation
- WINDOW 4.1 for the calculation of glazed designs

176–183 Experimental Cloud, Frankfurt/ Main (D) 2002 client: Messe Frankfurt GmbH

The objective was to construct a stable cloud as part of the special show "Constructing Atmospheres" at the exhibition Light & Building/Aircontec 2002. Twice a day inside the Galleria Frankfurt a several-hundred-cubic-meter-large cloud was to be generated from air layers of varying humidity and temperature. A climate engineer was to give a technical explanation of this process. At nightfall the Experimental Cloud would be transformed into an illuminated body hanging over the Cloud Club.

- Concept: Atelier Markgraph, Frankfurt/ Main with Transsolar, Stuttgart

Site factors
- Geographic position: latitude 50.12° north; longitude 8.68° east; elevation above sea level 113 m
- Mean outside temperature during the installation: 12°C
- Local ancillary conditions: located in the single-glazed linear atrium of the Galleria Frankfurt, a connecting wing between various exhibition spaces of the fairgrounds

Climate concept
- Generation of a stable temperature stratification by heating the atmosphere
- Fog formation through the introduction of saturated water vapor by spraying

Tools
- Laboratory measurements
- Measurements taken on-site from the 1:1 mock-up
- TRNSYS for thermal simulation
- FLUENT for transient air flow simulation

184–187 San Fermin housing project, Parcela 15, Madrid (E) 2003 client: EMV Empresa Municipal de la Vivienda, Madrid (E)

A seven-story residential building with 70 apartments in a very densely built neighborhood at the periphery of Madrid. The west façade is divided into sections and dominated by massive solar chimneys. The brief of this EU-sponsored architecture competition called for the use of solar energy to reduce the energy requirement for air conditioning and water heating. In keeping with the usual budget allotted for social housing projects the trend was toward simple integrated solutions rather than high-tech concepts.

- Architect: A.U.I.A. Arquitectos, Urbanistas, Ingenieros Asociados, Madrid (E)
- Structural engineer: IDEEE Ingenieria y Diseno de Estructuras Especiales de la Edificacion, Madrid (E)
- Energy consulting for client: Emilio Miguel Mitre, Madrid (E)
- Building physics: Manuel Marcias Miranda, University of Madrid (E)

Site factors
- Geographic position: longitude 40.40° north; latitude 25.75° west; elevation above sea level 612 m
- Solar irradiance (on horizontal surface per year) 1656 kWh/m²
- Humidity (1%) > 12.9 g/kg
- Local temperature conditions: minimum temperature -6.8°C; maximum temperature 38.9°C; average temperature of hottest month 24.3°C; mean annual temperature 13.9°C; temperature difference day/night during hottest month 16.2 K
- Local wind conditions: mean wind velocity (at 10 m) 2.4 m/s; main wind direction 170° (S); cool nighttime winds from the east
- Local ancillary conditions: densely built residential area at the periphery of the city; noise from the west due to proximity of a major road; east and west orientation of the main façades

Climate concept
- Making thermal storage mass available by modifying the ordinary ceiling construction
- East façade with glazed circulation galleries and supply air flaps
- Two-story apartments with air conduction via staircases
- West façade with vertical shading louvers and solar chimneys for removal of exhaust air
- Solar collectors for heating water

Tools
- Weather data analysis
- TRNSYS for thermal simulations and sizing of the solar chimneys
- Air flow simulation to test the ventilation system

188–199 New head office Deutsche Post AG, Bonn (D) 2002 client: Deutsche Post Bauen GmbH

A representative administration building with a forty-story, fully glazed office tower and a low-rise building situated near the Rhine. High demands on flexibility, increased workplace quality with natural lighting and ventilation, as well as user friendly elements, such as manually operable windows and limited individual control over heating and ventilation. Another objective was to reduce operating costs for heating, cooling, and ventilation by taking advantage of natural energy.

- Architect: Murphy/Jahn, Chicago (USA)
- Structural engineer: Werner Sobek Ingenieure, Stuttgart
- Building physics: Horstmann und Berger, Altensteig
- Building services: Brandi Consult, Köln-Berlin
- Artificial lighting: L-plan, Berlin

Site factors
- Geographic position: latitude 50.73° north; longitude 7.10° east; elevation above sea level 57 m
- Solar irradiance (on horizontal surface per year) 932 kWh/m²
- Humidity (1%) > 12.4 g/kg
- Local temperature conditions: minimum temperature -13.3°C; maximum temperature 33.4°C; average temperature of hottest month 17.4°C; mean annual temperature 9.6°C; temperature difference day/night during hottest month 11.0 K
- Local wind conditions: mean wind velocity (at 10 m) 3.1 m/s; main wind direction 180° (S)
- Local ancillary conditions: park-like environment in Rhine meadows; elliptical building form with east-west axis; surrounding buildings stand alone; high water table

Climate concept
- Double-skin façade with reflective solar protection
- Building component activation of the massive ceilings
- Cooling via groundwater wells
- Allow individual window ventilation to the double-skin façade
- Condition supply air to the offices via decentralized supply air units integrated into the façade
- Utilization of waste heat by directing exhaust air through the atria

Tools
- Weather data analysis
- TRNSYS for thermal simulations
- FIDAP for air flow simulations in and around the building
- Wind tunnel experiments
- COMIS for air flow simulations
- RADIANCE for daylight simulation
- 1:1 component testing of ventilation equipment
- 1:1 mock-up of two office floors including the double-skin façade

200–203 Refurbishing of Zeughaus for the Deutsches Historisches Museum, Berlin (D) 2003 client: Bundesamt für Bauwesen und Raumordnung

In the course of a general refurbishing of the Old Arsenal, a historical monument and seat of the German History Museum, the existing floors, ceilings, and windows are to be preserved according to the stipulations of monument conservation, and at the same time a modern climate and ventilation system is to be devised, which won't have visible ductwork and yet will provide full air conditioning of the rooms. The new, single-glazed roof of the inner courtyard, which has no shading, is to be a part of the climate concept.

- Architect: Winfried Brenne, Berlin
- Structural engineer: Pichler Ingenieure, Berlin
- Electrical planning: Werner Schwarz Ingenieure, Berlin
- HVAC and plumbing: Schreiber Ingenieure, Ulm

Site factors
- Geographic position: latitude 52.52° north; longitude 13.34° east; elevation above sea level 34 m
- Solar irradiance (on horizontal surface per year) 996 kWh/m²
- Humidity (1%) > 12.1 g/kg
- Local temperature conditions: minimum temperature -12.2°C; maximum temperature 33.8°C; average temperature of hottest month 17.9°C; mean annual temperature 8.7°C; temperature difference day/night during hottest month 9.3 K
- Local wind conditions: mean wind velocity (at 10 m) 4.1 m/s; main wind direction 202° (SSW)
- Local ancillary conditions: south side borders on a busy street, Unter den Linden; square plan with courtyard atrium, detached on three sides

Climate concept
- Double windows as air conduits, exhaust air is sucked out at a height of 5 meters and displacement supply air introduced in the occupied area
- Use of the radiator niches as installation surfaces for decentralized air conditioning units with the functions of providing fresh air, forced-air circulation heating and cooling, humidification and dehumidification

Tools
- TRNSYS for thermal simulations
- FIDAP for air flow simulations
- 1:1 component testing of ventilation equipment in the laboratories
- 1:1 test situation in the museum to measure data over an area of 200 m²

204–211 Renovation of the Tulane University student center, New Orleans (USA) 2004 client: Tulane University, New Orleans (USA)

The aim of refurbishing of the Student Center at Tulane University is to partially open the fully air-conditioned, hermetic building to the exterior. Under these climatic conditions comfort cannot be achieved via low room temperatures or minimizing humidity but rather one must resort to other factors such as radiant temperature, air velocity, and degree of turbulence.

- Architect: Vincent James Associates Architects, Minneapolis (USA) with James Carpenter Design Associates, New York (USA)
- Structural engineer: Kulkarni Consultants, New Orleans (USA)
- Façade: James Carpenter Design Associates Inc., New York (USA)
- Building services: Moses Engineers, New Orleans (USA)
- Daylighting: David Norris, New York (USA)

Site factors
- Geographic position: latitude 29.95° north, longitude 90.07° west; elevation above sea level 1 m
- Solar irradiance (on horizontal surface per year) 1656 kWh/m²
- Humidity (1%) > 20.7 g/kg
- Local temperature conditions: minimum temperature -6.3°C; maximum temperature 34.4°C; average temperature of hottest month 27.7°C; mean annual temperature 20.0°C; temperature difference day/night during hottest month 6.6 K
- Local wind conditions: mean wind velocity (at 10 m) 3.8 m/s; main wind direction 66° (E); to some extent complete lack of wind
- Local ancillary conditions: loosely structured university campus; main façades facing northeast, southeast, and southwest; extreme climatic conditions caused by abrupt shifts from rain to sun

Climate concept
- Raising air velocity and degree of turbulence with flap fans
- Limiting solar gains via shutters and parasol roof
- Radiant cooling and dehumidification via chilled water walls
- Solar chimney to enhance ventilation in situations with little wind
- Daylighting via skylights with diffusers

Tools
- Weather data analysis
- ASHRAE Thermal Comfort Program
- TRNSYS for thermal simulations
- FIDAP for air flow simulations
- 1:1 component testing of flap fans and water wall

212–221 Suvarnabhumi Airport, Bangkok (T) 2005 client: NBIA New Bangkok International Airport Co. Ltd., Bangkok (T)

With an area of 500,000 m² the new international airport in Bangkok will be one of the largest airports in the world. Hovering above the fully glazed terminal is a roof with louvers that will protect the room from sun and rain. A membrane system spans the entire 3.5-km-long concourse. The brief called for the development of a corresponding ventilation concept. Special demands included sound protection, natural lighting, and thermal comfort.

- Architect: MJTA Consortium with Murphy/Jahn, Chicago (USA); TAMS, Chicago (USA); ACT, Bangkok (T)
- Structural engineer: Werner Sobek Ingenieure, Stuttgart
- Building services: Flack and Kurtz Consulting Engineers, San Francisco (USA)
- Acoustics: Laboratorium für Optik und Dynamik, Leonberg

Site factors
- Geographic position: latitude 13.75° north; longitude 100.52° east; elevation above sea level 2 m
- Solar irradiance (on horizontal surface per year) 1752 kWh/m²
- Humidity (1%) > 22.9 g/kg
- Local temperature conditions: minimum temperature 16.3°C; maximum temperature 38.8°C; average temperature of hottest month 29.7°C; mean annual temperature 27.8°C; temperature difference day/night during hottest month 9.3 K
- Local wind conditions: mean wind velocity (at 10 m) 2.2 m/s; main wind direction 142° (SE)
- Local ancillary conditions: reclaimed swamp area; airplane noise; orientation of the building is indifferent; zenithal solar irradiation

Climate concept
- Exterior shading of the terminal roof
- Reduction of solar loads through the use of printed solar protection glass or membranes with extremely low radiation transmittance
- Cooling primarily via floor cooling, reducing air requirement for the displacement ventilation system
- Limitation of the conditioned air to the occupied zone
- Improvement of thermal comfort through thermal reflection off the inside ceiling surfaces

Tools
- Weather data analysis
- TRNSYS for thermal simulation
- FIDAP for air flow simulation
- RADIANCE for daylight simulation
- Laboratory measurements for material testing (membrane, glazing)
- 1:10 daylighting model
- 1:1 component testing of ventilation components

222–225 Mercedes-Benz Museum, Stuttgart (D) 2005 client: Grundstücksverwaltungsgesellschaft Mercedes-Benz AG & Co, OHG, Ludwigsfelde

A striking new museum building with a complex interior design for the documentation of the company's history. Inspired by automotive technology and design, the brief called explicitly for an innovative architectonic and technological concept. Other objectives were to minimize the engineered areas and mechanical building services. The idea was to ensure visitor comfort with limited energy input. High demands on combating glare and solar protection without sacrificing the view of the exterior.

- Architect: UN studio, van Berkel & Bos, Amsterdam (NL)
- Structural engineer: Werner Sobek Ingenieure, Stuttgart
- Façade: Arge DS-Plan, Stuttgart, Werner Sobek Ingenieure, Stuttgart
- Overall engineering: Transplan Technik-Bauplanung GmbH, Stuttgart with IB Schreiber, Ulm und IB Schwarz, Stuttgart
- Exhibition design: HG Merz, Stuttgart
- Artificial lighting: Ulrike Brandi Licht, Hamburg

Site factors
- Geographic position: latitude 48.76° north; longitude 9.18° east; elevation above sea level 359 m
- Solar irradiance (on horizontal surface per year) 1074 kWh/m²
- Humidity (1%) > 12.4 g/kg
- Local temperature conditions: minimum temperature -15.4°C; maximum temperature 33.2°C; average temperature of hottest month 18.3°C; mean annual temperature 9.1°C; temperature difference day/night during hottest month 10.8 K
- Local wind conditions: mean wind velocity (at 10 m) 2.5 m/s; main wind direction 250° (WSW)
- Local ancillary conditions: industrial area; location directly along a federal highway; level site in Neckartal; centralized layout

Climate concept
- HVAC controls centralized by floor to reduce ductwork
- Efficient ventilation and heat removal via displacement ventilation principle
- Building component cooling via floor and ceiling surfaces
- Air curtain to prevent cold air in lower levels
- Illumination of the traverse interior courtyard via mirrored deflection of sunlight

Tools
- Weather data analysis
- CAD diagrams of the altitude of the sun and shading projections
- TRNSYS for thermal simulations
- FIDAP for air flow simulations
- RADIANCE for daylight simulation
- 1:1 component testing of the illuminated ceiling with building component cooling

226–229 Museum of Tolerance, Jerusalem (IL) 2005 client: Simon Wiesenthal Center, Los Angeles (USA)

Geometrically complex new museum building with a conference center and theater as a place of learning. Three fully glazed areas, atrium, cafeteria, and theater lobby, are to be protected from overheating without compromising their transparency and at the same time minimizing the energy input and operating costs for air conditioning.

- Architect: Frank O. Gehry and Associates, Los Angeles (USA)
- Special construction glazed roofs: Schlaich Bergermann und Partner, Stuttgart
- Building services: Cosentini Associates, New York (USA); Assa Aharoni Consulting Engineers, Tira Carmel (IL); Karel Valent; Tel Aviv (IL)
- Project supervision: Eliezer Rahat, Jerusalem (IL)

Site factors
- Geographic position: latitude 31.77° north; longitude 35.23° east; elevation above sea level 744 m
- Solar irradiance (on horizontal surface per year) 2094 kWh/m²
- Humidity (1%) > 14.8 g/kg
- Local temperature conditions: minimum temperature -0.8°C; maximum temperature 36.4°C; average temperature of hottest month 23.3°C; mean annual temperature 16.1°C; temperature difference day/night during hottest month 10.2 K
- Local wind conditions: mean wind velocity (at 10 m) 4.7 m/s; main wind direction 285° (W)
- Local ancillary conditions: heightened security demands against terrorist attacks; rocky ground, no groundwater; atrium oriented lengthwise from north to south, cafeteria on the south side of the museum with roof overhang

Climate concept
- Roof overhangs made of printed glass as fixed solar protection
- Vertical roof extension to prevent heat accumulation in the occupied zone
- Glass roof made of highly selective, printed solar protection glass with a low-e coating on the inside layer
- Floor cooling on the ground floor and in the galleries
- Natural ventilation via façade flaps
- Displacement ventilation in the cafeteria and theater lobby

Tools
- Weather data analysis
- TRNSYS for thermal simulations
- FLUENT for air flow simulations and analysis of smoke removal
- RADIANCE for daylight simulation in the atrium
- Sampling of large-format glass panes with various printed patterns

Edited by
Anja Thierfelder
Technical editor and glossary
Thomas Lechner
Concept
Wilfried Korfmacher
Anja Thierfelder
Andreas Uebele
Layout and typesetting
Büro Uebele
Visuelle Kommunikation
Katrin Häfner
Andreas Uebele
Christine Voshage
Photo
Frank O. Gehry and Associates (226, 228)
Archiv Werner Sobek; Photos: Gabriela Heim, ILEK (212/213, 216/217, 220/221, 224)
Anja Thierfelder (12–202)
Rendering
Murphy/Jahn architects (214/215, 218/219)
UN studio, van Berkel & Bos (222)
Vincent James Associates Architects with James Carpenter Design Associates
(204/205, 206, 208, 210)
English proofreading
Andrew Leslie
Translation
Kimi Lum
Repro
C+S Repro
Printer
Leibfarth & Schwarz
Binder
Riethmüller
Typeface
Akzidenz Grotesk bold, bold italic
Paper
Samat Römerturm 180/280/150 g

A CIP catalogue record for this book is available from the Library of Congress, Washington D.C., USA

Bibliographic information published by Die Deutsche Bibliothek

Die Deutsche Bibliothek lists this publication in the Deutsche Nationalbibliografie; Detailed bibliographic data is available in the Internet at http://dnb.ddb.de.

This book has also been published in a German language edition (ISBN 3-7643-0792-7)

©2003 Birkhäuser – Publishers for Architecture, P.O. Box 133, CH-4010 Basel, Switzerland
Part of Springer Science + Business Media
Printed on acid-free paper produced from chlorine-free pulp. TCF
Printed in Germany

ISBN 3-7643-0751-X

9 8 7 6 5 4 3 2 1